Dog Tags

&

Wedding Bands

by

Joe Rosato

DORRANCE
PUBLISHING CO
EST. 1920
PITTSBURGH, PENNSYLVANIA 15238

Dorrance Publishing Co
585 Alpha Drive
Pittsburgh, PA 15238
Visit our website at *www.dorrancebookstore.com*

ISBN: 978-1-4809-5135-8
eISBN: 978-1-4809-5111-2

This book is dedicated
to all the women civilians who volunteered
to serve their country
in the Vietnam War.
We as a nation owe you so much more than just a thank you.

**A special thank you to two people
whom without their many hours of hard work
this book would not have been published.**

Maureen Mallon
for proof reading and editing
my sometimes lost thoughts into proper language.

&

Gina Rosato
for creating the striking story telling book cover and photo design.
gina@creativecrackerjack.com

Prologue

Did you know that thousands of women played an active role in the Vietnam War? Sadly their roles have been mostly forgotten. According to independent surveys, between 33,000 and 55,000 women took part in the war in both military active duty and civilian roles. Even as women strived for equality, they were treated like second-class soldiers in the military and also after they came home. Most of the women who served in Vietnam were nurses, but they were not properly trained for dealing with the combat injuries they would come across. The enemies used artilleries that were specifically made to inflict massive injuries. Besides the weapons, there were napalm, white phosphorous, and antipersonnel bombs. Once helicopters were used to airlift wounded soldiers to hospitals, this meant that the nurses saw more vicious wounds compared to previous wars and even more soldiers required treatment.

It still isn't clear, even to this day, how many civilian women volunteered during the Vietnam War. Our country should have paid closer attention to tracking the numbers, but they didn't and ultimately brushed the task aside. Numerous women volunteered for organizations like The American Red Cross, Peace Corps, and the USO. Some also volunteered as missionaries and journalists, and none of them should ever be forgotten.

Similarly to the men who were heading to Vietnam to serve their country, young women volunteered from every possible background and mostly served as nurses in hospitals and medical facilities in South Vietnam. They volunteered for several reasons: service to their country, to help wounded servicemen, to get education and training, to advance their careers in the military, to prove themselves, or simply as an adventure. Nurses served on Navy hospital ships, on the Air Force's airlift helicopters, and airplanes as well as the Army's hospitals. They had a range of experience when they arrived in Vietnam, from newcomers to veterans with years of service. The inexperienced quickly became experienced due to the stress and the sheer number of casualties they had to deal with. Even with the long hours and horrific wounds they hand to deal with, many of these nurses somehow still found fulfillment in serving others.

Women known as "The Donut Dollies" volunteered through Supplemental Recreation Activities Overseas (SRAO) which was a program ran by the American Red Cross. Sometimes they were called "Chopper Chicks" and "Kool-Aid Kids."

Irrespective of what they were called, cheering up the troops was their mission, even though their lives were in danger every day. Even with their service and sacrifice, their contributions and stories seem to have faded away.

Eight women were killed while in the Vietnam war while serving in the military. You can find their names on the Vietnam Veterans Memorial Wall in Washington, D.C., however, they are overshadowed by over 58,000 names of men. Only 1st Lt. Sharon Ann Lane died due to hostile fire when she was killed in Chu Lai by a rocket attack. Plane crashes or being in the wrong place at the wrong time killed the other seven women.

Approximately 59 civilian volunteers were also killed during the Vietnam War, but sadly they are not mentioned when talking about the Vietnam War casualties. Keep in mind that these women served on the battlefront as there were no front lines, and they were surrounded by enemies. In the face of this constant danger, the nurses never stopped showing compassion, care, and dedication.

"No event in American history is more misunderstood than the Vietnam War. It was misreported then, and it is misremembered now. Rarely have so many people been so wrong about so much. Never have the consequences of their misunderstanding been so tragic." … Richard Nixon

This is a fictional story and all names, places, and dates used by the author are both factual and non-factual. Bringing attention to the brave civilian women was the main purpose of writing this book. They didn't have to go to war, but they went and faced the danger anyway. Keep in mind that volunteers were treated the same as soldiers, sailors, and airmen who served in Vietnam when they returned home without any parades. They were also spat upon and cursed at on their return home and were discriminated against when seeking employment.

Our country has never recognized or acknowledged the critical contributions these volunteer women made and who gave up so much in the defense of this nation. They did not escape the horrors of post-traumatic stress disorder (PTSD) and had to readjust to civilian life without any government assistance.

My personal Navy service in the Vietnam War has helped the story line and contributed to the story's content. I hope that someday soon we, as a nation, will pause just for a moment and properly thank these amazing women who gave unwavering and selfless service and never asked for anything in return.

Chapter 1

1972 Havre de Grace, MD

There she was, sitting on a rusted trailer, front and center on a lawn in Joppa-towne. The young couple were returning from a short getaway weekend at the Inner Harbor in Baltimore. She was full of dead leaves and rainwater, a fiberglass relic of the 1950's; her paint was faded but still had deep pennant blue tones. Her finish, from bumper to bumper, was laced with hairline cracks. He fell in love at first sight.

What Chet saw was a 1954 Corvette convertible that could be his very own. A sleek well-rounded design which gave him the feeling of the classic European race cars of its day, ready to take him wherever he steered her. What his wife, Nancy, saw was a needy addition to the family. But she didn't ban the purchase, and in his wisdom, he never asked her to help him clean or work on it.

Chet owned the Corvette for eight years paying along the way for numerous repairs such as a muffler system, brakes, radiator, tires, springs/shocks, and even a new convertible top. He probably drove it for less than a thousand miles total over the eight years. Realizing that the car was a black hole in the family finances, he sold it for about half of what he put into it.

Chet recounted those days when he and Nancy would take long rides in that old 1954 relic. Driving along the winding roads and rural hills of Western Maryland with the top down made Chet feel as though he was Mario Andretti. Catching a quick glance of Nancy's flowing brunette locks in the wind would make the view through Chet's eyes priceless. Nancy was always a good sport about the expense of trying to upgrade the car, and she never once brought it up in any conversation.

2005 Kiawah Island, SC

The lonely drive back from the cemetery to his home in Kiawah Island without the love of his life is slowly taking its toll on him. Situated on a barrier island, his home was the place he and Nancy were going to spend their retirement years together. Chet had just retired and their well laid out plans were now disintegrating before his eyes. Stopping at the foot of his driveway, taking in the view of their beautiful ocean front home sends streaks of anger, causing him to pound on the steering wheel of his car with fury. Chet cries out, "All this hard work, and no one to share it with."

Nancy was an only child of William and Elizabeth Noonan of Bel Air, MD. Born on July 7th, 1949, she was a quick learner in school and wanted to be a veterinary technician. Her parents, of modest means, sent her to the Community College of Baltimore. Nancy received her two-year degree and began working at veterinary offices in and around the greater Baltimore area. Once she met Chet, the dreams of furthering her education to become a veterinarian came to a halt.

The burial service was held at Bethany Cemetery in Charleston, SC where Chet placed Nancy to rest. His children wanted him to bury their mother up north, in Havre de Grace, MD where they grew up and most of the family's friends lived. Chet's explanation of their mother's love for Charleston persuaded them to agree with him. Placing his key in the keyhole of a now empty home leads Chet to walk directly over to the well-stocked built-in bar. Grabbing a bottle of his favorite Jack Daniel's Green Label and his silver trim rock glass, Chet makes his way to the sliding doors. Stepping out on the deck and sliding over a lounge chair, Chet settles in and pours the warm spirts over ice with a lemon twist.

Nancy and Chet were proud parents of Chester Jr. and Cathy who are both married with children. Chester and his wife, Ann, live in Morgantown, WV and have a 9-year-old daughter, Amy. Chet's daughter Cathy and her husband, Carl Schmitt, have two children, Neil, 11 years and Amanda 8-years-old, and they reside in York, PA.

Hallways, fireplace mantels, and furniture tops filled with family photos remind Chet of all the memories of Nancy. Reaching all the way back to their dating days when she first caught his eye at a party held at a friend's house in Glen Burnie, MD. It was in 1967 when Chet recently joined the Navy they quickly became good friends. In six months they were engaged, and they married in July. Nancy became a housewife with the arrival of their first child, Cathy, born in September of 1971. A year and a half later, their second child, Chester, was born in February of 1973. Recollections of the family spending their weekends and vacations on the Delmarva Peninsula flash by in Chet's memory. Family fishing and crabbing trips to Crystal Beach reflect the best of times, especially when Nancy packed her famous lunches. Nancy always considered having the best of meals when they day tripped.

Some of her favorite menu items included Greek salad wraps, baguette sandwiches, Italian pasta salad, and cinnamon picnic cake. This all made a bad day of catching fish or crabs into a great day to have fun and feast on her homemade gourmet lunches.

Along the main hallway, there's a picture of Nancy holding the biggest blue claw crab Chet had ever seen. The giant crab's main shell measured 7 1/2 inches tip to tip. Nancy used a drop line and chicken necks as bait instead of Chet's preferred fish heads. Chet remembered telling Nancy her choice of bait would never work. About five minutes later, she felt a tugging pull on her drop line and had difficulty pulling it in. Chet remarked that her drop line must be stuck on something. Nancy was determined to bring the drop line in even though her hands were hurting from the line cutting into them. When the catch came to the surface of the water, Chet immediately noticed it was a giant blue claw crab. He ran for the net and slowly tried to scoop it from underneath. The crab's claw reach was bigger than his net and luckily, the crab grabbed onto the netting so it could be brought in.

Chet and Nancy's goal wasn't to live high on the hog, so they strived to achieve a modest lifestyle that mattered to both. By plotting a course of financial freedom, their dreams could be lived in retirement. Penny pinching in the early years of their marriage made it all possible when the time came, sooner than later, in life. Nancy tried to contribute to the family finances by working part time at a local veterinary hospital. She loved animals and enjoyed her job immensely. There were times when abused stray cats and dogs were dropped off at the hospital after being picked up at roadside by the police. There were many times when Nancy would bring the animals home, especially on long weekends, because she felt that no abused animal should be alone. Nancy worked very hard to find new homes for those animals and would always check out the potential new home by herself before the animal was handed over. Driving one hundred miles out of the way was always worthwhile in her mind. Nancy had such a firm conviction on checking out a new home for an animal; she had to be one hundred percent confident that her placements were long-term.

Every now and then, special vacation plans came up for discussion, and Nancy would do all the leg work to find things for them to do. She was particularly fond of Cadillac Mountain on Mt. Desert Island, ME located within the Acadia National Park. The views from Cadillac Mountain were always spectacular, particularly at sunrise and sunset. They would drive over from the main land while bringing a bottle of chardonnay wine and toast each sunrise and sunset of their vacation. While on Cadillac Mountain, there were many times during sunsets, being so peaceful and tranquil, that they would dose off cuddling each other as the sun fell into its resting place over the horizon.

Tears begin to run down Chet's cheeks while his heart rumbles at an irregular beat causing an uncontrollable whimpering shiver. His emotional state of mind is in total disarray making him feel helpless and without purpose. Chet's first lonely night and several subsequent nights are sleepless. The simple function of sleep doesn't come naturally while he tosses and turns in bed with his mind wandering. Facing Nancy's side of the bed carries strong visions of her lying next to him. Chet envisions her staring at him as she lightly strokes his face and moving her lips as though she wanted to say something.

After a few weeks of building the courage, Chet starts to go through Nancy's things. Opening shoe boxes, going through handbags, jewelry boxes, and coat pockets. His searching leads him to find small amounts of cash, broken earrings, and various personal items. Each of Nancy perfumes are opened and sniffed. As he reads the labels, he recounts an intimate moment between them. The names of L'air Du Temps, with its white dove as a bottle top, and Shalimar's blue shell top are rediscovered. This all reminds him of Nancy spritzing the bed pillows with perfume whenever she changed the sheets.

Hanger by hanger, Chet holds and smells each piece of clothing as he conveys a past moment back to life. The satin blue dress, almost the exact color of their Corvette, reminds him of a time when she first wore it. It was a New Year's Eve party at the end of 1999, and the arrival of a new millennium. The talk of the party was all about computers and the internet failing at the stroke of midnight. Nancy and Chet were of only a select few who believed nothing would happen, but it was Nancy who convinced the crowd that nothing would change. When the new year arrived, someone turned on their computer and announced that all was a go. Almost all the attendees immediately thanked Nancy as though it was all her making.

His goal was to donate her clothing items, but he stumbles upon items he never knew existed. A hand-written label in Nancy's unique handwriting style catches Chet's eye while he is bending over a pile of shoes. The markings read "Letters," which stops him in his tracks and stimulates his curiosity. As he opens the large boot box, he finds that it was being used for storing all the letters between them while he was overseas serving in Vietnam. He had no idea whatsoever that she kept all their letters, and he wondered why. Also in the box, he hears a rattling sound when it was lifted. In the corner of the box, Chet feels for what was rattling and touches three long rounded objects. The first item he grabbed turned out to be an Esterbrook silver fountain pen, which Chet visually inspects. He continues using his fingers to sift through the letters and finds two more similar objects, but this time they both turn out to be Sheaffer fountain pens. During a closer inspection, he remembers all Nancy's letters to him were written in longhand by fountain pens. The pens were given to her by her mother who used them during the 1940's when she wrote to her father in WWII. Nancy and her mother especially cherished the Esterbrook because of its silver nibs, which required far less wrist effort than a ballpoint. Both Nancy and her mom both claimed that it was the preferred brand of pen, used by Abraham Lincoln when he penned his famous speeches.

Fiddling through one letter at a time, scanning post mark dates, he came across a letter written when he first arrived in Vietnam. The letter was post marked February 4, 1968, and in that letter, he reads his own account of his arrival in Saigon. Page two of his letter hit home as he read out loud:

> "Sitting twenty rows back at a window seat of a Boeing 707, I noticed an orderly long line of mostly Army personnel waiting on the ground off to the side of our plane. Without a peep, the entire plane emptied, each a young clean-cut military person, in somewhat pressed uniforms, displaying a look of surprise with wide open eyes. We all neatly followed our instructions to closely follow the person in front of us down the aisle, stairs, and on to the ground. We assembled just to the side under a wing of the plane. We were called to attention by the Master Sergeant in charge. It was explained to us that the seasoned group boarding the plane had just finished their tours of duty and were on their way home. As the seasoned group got closer, we were all shocked to see

how tired and war torn they looked. Those guys were all wearing shabby looking uniforms that showed heavy use. Most displayed longer hair, mustaches, and a couple of weeks of facial hair growth. Our group of arrivals stopped while the war-torn guys walked by us. Not one of them looked at us or made a comment. With a look of being to hell and back, it was very odd that no returning veteran smiled or showed any sign of happiness, even though they were on the way home. It made me think of how lucky they were to be going home, when someone standing next to me whispered, 'Look at the caskets stacked by the C-130. I guess they're going home too.'"

Chet is a quiet man who always kept his personal life outside of normal conversation with friends, and only his closest family members knew of his Navy service. He never talked about his Vietnam war experience nor did he ever wear ball caps, shirts, or patches announcing the fact that he was a veteran. Sometimes Chet wished he could be more like the freewheeling motorcycle Vietnam vets who were proud to talk about their experiences during the war. But he felt his time in Vietnam was more than wearing a leather jacket filled with patches. Inside his heart, he was as proud as hell for serving his country. Those feelings were something no one could ever take away. Reading his old letters reminded Chet of how surreal each day that he spent in Vietnam was. During his tour of duty, he witnessed things which made sense at the time, but make no sense now. He sadly recalled how the outrageous was accepted as normal.

Picking one of Nancy's letters was a little harder to find a certain postmark date since she wrote at least four times more often than Chet. Settling on one letter sent by Nancy, in a pink envelope that still had a perfume scent when it was handled. The beautiful longhand lettering reminded Chet as if he were reading a letter written in calligraphy. It was a long letter, so he settles on the third paragraph:

"Oh, Chet, our Thanksgiving table is so beautiful. Mom and I handmade a centerpiece using pine cones, wild berries, nuts, and Indian corn dressed around a pumpkin. I've taken some pictures, and I will send them to you when the film is developed. Our menu today is turkey (of course) with sausage stuffing, mashed potatoes with brown gravy, string beans, and homemade cranberry sauce. For dessert, we have a pumpkin pie and whipped cream that I made myself. It took a second attempt since my first pie burnt in the oven. Ha Ha! Hope you are well and in a safe place. I miss you very much and love you with all my heart."

Nancy's letters were always filled with joy and happiness. Her writings constantly made Chet feel as though he was still with her, standing by her side, even though he was halfway around the world. Her letters also had hidden inside small trinkets, newspaper articles, photos, and gag jokes. Once a month, Nancy would send a package filled with cans of fruit, tuna fish, pudding, and apple sauce. Chet recounts the fond memories of sharing those packaged goodies with his crew members.

Under the amber moon of August 23^{rd,} a large tropical depression began to form over the Bahamas. From an intersection between a tropical wave, remnants of Tropical Depression Ten made the potential birth of a named hurricane. In the early morning of August 24^{th,} the eleventh named storm, Hurricane Katrina, and the fifth hurricane of the 2005 announcing the Atlantic hurricane season is born. Unknown at the time, the storm will become the costliest natural disaster as well as one of the five deadliest hurricanes in the history of the United States.

Over the next few days, Chet watches cable news channels give blow by blow details of the storm twisting and turning towards an unknown point of contact. On August 28th, Katrina is upgraded to a level five storm. August 29th, New Orleans is hit with a flood surge which compromised its levees, giving way to flooding waters which submerged eighty percent of the city.

Reading those old letters rekindled Chet's desire to see some of his old Navy buddies. He certainly now has the time to see his old friends. He began to reminisce about how Nancy would sometimes suggest calling them to get together. Having a reunion now with his crew members would settle two accomplishments in his life. First, seeing his old crew members after all these years and secondly, carrying out Nancy's wishes.

Meanwhile trying to rekindle some old friendships with a get together is easier said than done. In calling his former crew members, Chet discovers that the long distances between his friends, along with their serious medical conditions, makes a get together almost impossible. While connecting with his shipmates, Chet stumbles upon the fact that he is the only one not being treated for any effects of Agent Orange. The thought of being the only one not effected is bewildering, but he wishes his friends the best, hoping it all will work out.

Chet Ross recently retired after a very successful career in corporate insurance sales. He and his wife retired to Kiawah Island, leaving their long-time residence in Havre de Grace, MD which is situated at the mouth of the Susquehanna River and the head of Chesapeake Bay. During his working career, Chet traveled extensively and during those years, he was often on the road making sales calls from coast to coast.

He is also a former Navy veteran with service during the Tet Offensive. In late January 1968 during the lunar new year (or "Tet") holiday, North Vietnamese and communist Viet Cong forces launched a coordinated attack against several targets in South Vietnam. The United States and South Vietnamese militaries sustained heavy loses before finally repelling the assault. The first Tet Offensive played an important role in weakening U.S. public support for the war in Vietnam. Although the first phase of the offensive became the most famous, a second phase also launched simultaneous assaults on smaller cities and towns on May 4th and stretched into June. A third phase began in August and lasted six weeks. In the months that followed, U.S. and South Vietnamese forces retook the towns that the communist's forces had secured over the course of the offensive, but they incurred heavy military and civilian casualties in the process.

Chet served on a Patrol Craft Fast, (PCF-33) also known as a Swift Boat, they were all-aluminum, 50-foot long, shallow-draft vessels operated by the United States Navy initially to patrol the coastal areas and later for work in the interior waterways as part of the brown-water-Navy to interdict Viet Cong movement of arms and munitions, transport Vietnamese forces. Serving on a swift boat was a match made in heaven for Chet. His vast seamanship experience while living and working in the Chesapeake Bay as a teenager gave him the ability to fit in like a glove.

In 1965 the Navy devised the swift boat idea to create a craft that was reliable, non-wooden hull, 500-mile range, speed 25 knots, high-resolution radar, long range communications, quiet running, small armament, sparse berthing, no cooking, swallow water ability, and a powerful searchlight. During the Vietnam War, swift boats main purpose was to patrol and stop Viet Cong movement of arms and munitions, transport forces, and insert specially trained teams for counterinsurgency.

He was a gunner's mate, third class, and had many close encounters with death during fire fights along the Mekong Delta rivers. Chet was especially proud of his Purple Heart Medal awarded for taking a bullet fragment in his left thigh which was stopped by his femur bone. Chet was also awarded a Bronze Star and PCF-33, and his entire crew of six received the Navy Unit Commendation. During many times PCF-33 was attached to support The US Army 9th Infantry Division and their operations.

Chet's intensive nine week training to become a swift boat crew member began in Coronado, CA. The rigorous training covered fitness, swimmer skills, first aid, maritime navigation, seamanship, engineering, communication, weapons, and special warfare. His official Navy title was a "Gunners Mate," and his main function was to man a .50 caliber machine gun, but also maintain the ability to step into the shoes of any other crew member if needed. Knowing all the boat's functions and operations was a prerequisite for duty. In addition a "Gunners Mate" had to master a breech loading mortar and agent orange sprayer attachments. Agent orange was used and sprayed along the river banks by swift boats. This allowed the swift boats to have some distance from possible sniper fire in tree tops and dense brush.

PCF-33 was a special swift boat that had a war dog and trainer attached to the crew. The trainer's name was Petty Officer Second Class Ruggero DiMucci who was from Trenton, NJ, and his dog was a Chocolate Lab named Buck. Ruggero DiMucci's nickname was "Rugby." He earned the name because of his fearless ability to run into harm's way while most ran from harm's way. During a nasty fight when he was a teenager, Rugby's face was slashed with a knife, and his nose was broken. His family couldn't afford to pay the medical costs, so he learned to live with the face of a British Rugby Player, scarred and battered. Growing up as a kid in the Italian section of Trenton gave Rugby his fearless attitude which he carried with him to Vietnam.

In April of 1966, the US Navy started to experiment with the use of War Dogs on its small craft vessels which would eventually evolve into swift boats. At first German shepherds were used, but they didn't have strong enough swimming abilities. The Navy decided to use Labrador Retrievers because of their webbed paws which made them excellent swimmers. Labs were predominately trained as tracker dogs with a mission to locate the enemy, but not engage. But history now shows that labs did in fact engage with enemy forces. The use of labs instead of shepherds made the job of the trainer more fitting for in or on the water surveillance versus using an attack dog. Having a lab as part of the PCF-33 crew provided them with the added advantage of the lab's keen hearing, sight, and smell.

Chet as a boy loved dogs, but his parents never wanted to have one, even though he promised them on countless occasions to take care of it. Maybe it was because of his childhood wish of always wanting a dog that Chet developed a solid bond with Buck. Buck loved to have his underbelly rubbed, and Chet would always take the time to make him happy. Chet and Buck grew to have a special bond in which they always seemed to look out for one another. However, there were times when Rugby seemed to act strangely toward Chet's relationship with Buck saying to Chet, "You're getting in the way of Buck's special training, so stop it!"

In a real way, spending time on a boat was nothing new to Chet. During his summer vacations, while in high school, Chet spent many summers working on fishing charter boats that trolled the Chesapeake Bay. The size of a 50-foot swift boat was about the size of the charter boats he worked on while he learned thorough seamanship. Through the summers of 1963 and 1964, Chet spent his time working on a 52-foot commercial fishing boat that was converted to be used as a ferry. Based out of Crisfield, MD, the "Black Whale" ran scheduled shuttles to Smith Island, MD. The island's only means of connecting with the mainland was by boat. The Black Whale ran every two hours starting at 10 am until 6 pm, seven days a week, delivering vacationers and day trippers to the historic Chesapeake Bay island. The work schedule was grueling, and Chet only had Wednesdays off since it was the slowest day of the week for the Black Whale. The seamanship experience learned by Chet was priceless. Captain Rumble, who was also the boat owner, ran a skeleton crew each Wednesday leaving himself to work a full seven-day week. During the winter months, the Black Whale travelled south to Islamorada, FL in the Florida Keys where Captain Rumble offered sunset cruises to vacationers. Chet always considered Captain Rumble a mentor and one of the hardest working people he ever met. Chet always tried in his work life to emulate Captain Rumble's high-level labor ethics.

Each day the hurricane progress was getting worse as news agencies report the flooding caused by washed away levees in the wake of Katrina. To most of the television audience the term "storm surge" becomes a new phrase in the media mantra. While Chet hears all the hurricane reports, it has him recall his service in Vietnam in 1968 when an unknown tropical depression developed in the South China sea. On September 13th, 1968, that tropical depression rapidly turned into a full fledge typhoon. Hitting the mainland causing havoc on the entire Mekong Delta area. The troublesome typhoon was the third storm of that season which was named Typhoon Cobra by navy command in Honolulu. Typhoon Cobra was unpredictable and originally tracked to stay in the Southern Pacific, but at the last moment made a westerly turn directly toward Vietnam. Navy Command only had an eighteen-hour warning window for Mekong Delta forces. "Typhoon Cobra" sent a wall of water measuring over fifteen-feet, surging up into all the rivers and small tributaries. Tiny villages not only had to worry about the Viet Cong wiping them out, but now Mother Nature also took her toll.

The great storm was responsible for killing thousands of people who never received any warning. Villages as far away as ten miles from rivers were engulfed with flooding walls of water. South Vietnam's wetlands are mostly at or below sea-level making it a perfect place to grow rice, but a not so perfect place during a tidal surge. The government only issued limited weather reports for the larger cities leaving the small towns and villages on their own. Even if the government knew of the oncoming force that Typhoon Cobra carried, attempting to get a warning to the hundreds of small villages would have been an impossible task. Local officials had no way to communicate with the fishermen and rice farmers in the Mekong Delta causing the innocent men, women, and children to pay with their lives.

Chet knew damn well that a storm surge was a costal flood or tsunami-like phenomenon of rising water, commonly associated with a low-pressure weather systems. His training recalled measuring the severity of a storm by the shallowness of the body of water in the path of the storm. Adding in the timing of high tides, a full moon, and wind direction pushing water onshore made for a perfect storm surge. Chet also knew that most casualties during a hurricane or typhoon occurred because of storm surge. Hurricane Katrina news reporting was too like that of Typhoon Cobra giving Chet an uncomfortable feeling as he closely listened to the similarities.

Recalling Typhoon Cobra heading west toward Cambodia after battering southern Vietnam with powerful winds and heavy rain, leaving behind nothing but destruction. The official death toll in Vietnam was placed at about 1,000, but officials said that number was expected to rise as more reports came in and as the floodwaters threatened further destruction. Chet never did receive the final death toll due to his swift boat being returned to duty status shortly after the storm passed.

Chet remembers the rain was heavy and the wind was so forceful, it was as though it had a mind of its own. Shortly after the storm passed, the sun was shining brightly; there were nothing but white clouds and blue skies. Chet's recalling the clear weather was deceptive and the dangers had not passed. Typhoon Cobra became the most serious typhoon that ever hit the country of Vietnam. Once again Chet listened very closely to the same Hurricane Katrina resemblance of peace and calm followed by flooding waters.

As Chet reminisced about hearing reports from Saigon, river levels rose even higher from rain rushing down the mountain sides that added to the already record-level flooding. Weather reports stated the flood waters surpassed the historic highs of a 1964 unnamed storm when most of Vietnam, Laos, Cambodia, were ravaged leaving thousands of dead and millions homeless.

Fortunately Typhoon Cobra was already weakening as it headed toward Laos weather stations reported. Hearing the good news that the storm was expected to completely dissipate over land within the next 12 hours as it continued to track to the west gave Chet a feeling of relief.

The damage in central Vietnam was far less than in the southern region where the typhoon was reported to have caused the most deaths and inundated the homes of millions of people. To make matters even worse, Chet recalls hearing that cyclones were being reported along the Mekong Delta area. Those same reports admitted that they were used to storms that sweep away within a few hours, but never saw a storm that strong last so long. In comparison Hurricane Katrina reports also signaled to Chet its lasting effects now causing worries about the New Orleans Levies holding back Lake Pontchartrain.

Official typhoon reports said the central highlands region was experiencing flash floods and mud slides killing an estimated 150 and causing serious damage to the country's coffee growing industry. Flooding receded over the next few days in the ancient cities of Hue and Hoi An allowing most of the old buildings to withstand yet another storm onslaught and continue to stand firm until the next typhoon.

During the typhoon, many foreign volunteers and news reporters had been trapped in Hoi An, some doubling up in hotel rooms as water rose on the lower floors. Others were sequestered in hotels out in Da Nang. Vietnamese television showed reporters and other Westerners in rain coats wading through the waist-deep water in Hoi An filming their reports.

Typhoon Cobra also destroyed crops, irrigation systems, and livestock. Farmers were left with nothing, and their farming landscape was totally washed away. The powers of Mother Nature left the poor even poorer. After the storm passed military flyovers, showed vast brown oceans with rooftops, and trees poking above the water. Whatever powerlines were in place before the storm were now ripped away by wind and rushing waters filled with debris.

In Da Nang, the country's fourth largest city, damage appeared relatively light given the force of the storm with fallen trees scattered on the streets and electric lines down, but with houses and roofs intact according to witnesses and television footage.

Television stations broadcast images of Allied Forces and uniformed officials delivering food supplies to people huddled in damp and darkened homes, their faces lighted by flashlights as they thanked the government for its help.

After Typhoon Cobra rescinded its force on the local population, Navy swift boats were ordered back into the rivers to survey the damages. While performing reconnaissance missions, Chet began to hear strange gurgling sounds. Chet was the only person on board the swift boat who heard the gurgling sounds, and his crew members began to think his reactions were odd. Due to the storm surge, all the rivers in the Mekong Delta area developed many new sand and mud bars. This made traveling in the rivers very hazardous which resulted in the boats moving at slower speeds. Until the sand/mud bars were dredged, the swift boats suddenly became easy targets for the enemy.

Attempting to take his mind off the 24/7 coverage of Katrina, Chet tries to rejuvenate his seascape painting talents. It's been more than thirty years since he even held an artist brush in his hand. Reading through some of his old art publications, he comes across his favorite artist, Robert Wood, who was an American landscape painter born in England and who rose to prominence in the 1950's. The famous artist settled in California, making Monterey and Laguna Beach his favorite places to paint. These beautiful locations offered Robert Wood the rocky coast and pounding surf that made his paintings come to life.

The Robert Wood book is called *How to Paint Seascapes* in a magazine format printed in color. Skimming through the pages, Chet comes across a seascape he copied in 1963 as a teenager. He tries to remember whatever happened to his copy of the painting, but can't remember where he might have placed it. After searching all the places where it might have been, he gives up trying to find it and decides to, once again, duplicate the painting. But he finds out very quickly that the enjoyment of painting during his teenage years has vanished. The basic skill of holding a paint brush doesn't feel the same, and his once steady hand no longer exists.

Trying to move on to something new and different, Chet begins woodworking projects and making repairs around his house. Weeks of painting and sanding don't give him any sense of accomplishment and just lead to boredom. Never giving up, but still looking for that hobby which will give him a feeling of achievement, Chet tries to learn the horticulture world of flowers and vegetables. The warm climate of South Carolina offers an extended growing season. Chet begins to experiment and tries growing exotic flowers such as birds of paradise, trumpet vine and various types of orchids. Chet finds that this new hobby takes too much of his time and involves a labor of love. The hard work of pruning, graphing, fertilizing overcome his enjoyment. The beauty of watching his garden grow begins to wane and with it, all his enjoyment. Chet gives serious thought to buying a chocolate lab fulfilling his children's dream, but decides to put it off until he is firmly set in what his future will be. The last thing Chet wants is to be homebound with a dog if he decides to travel.

Early on a Wednesday morning, before the sun was up, Chet is awakened by an odd mild pain in his abdominal area. It's a throbbing pain that seems to come and go every ten minutes. Chet self-diagnoses the pain is a result of anxiety and must have something to do with the pressure and a side effect of losing his wife. But just to play it safe, he decides to call Dr. Carter and makes a quick appointment to visit the office. The examination is general, and Dr. Carter can't determine what is causing the intermittent pulses of pain. The doctor recommends various tests be done and asks Chet if he will seek medical care at the VA Hospital in Charleston. Chet explains that he would never go back to the VA again since his last misdiagnosis. He explains that almost two years ago, the VA misdiagnosed a respiratory infection as lung cancer. If it wasn't for Nancy noticing that the x-rays did not belong to him, radiation and chemo treatments would have commenced. Even before his treatment, Chet had conversations with other veterans who had nothing but horror stories to report. Some of those stories included long waits for treatment, lack of proper medication, and a veteran having his teeth pulled and having to wait months for his replacement teeth. Without any surprised expression on his face Doctor Carter sets up a series of test at Roper Medical Center in Charleston.

After returning from the doctor, Chet turns his thoughts away from worrying about negative test results. But eerily Chet begins dreaming of an old dream he hasn't had for over thirty-five years. The dreams begin to occur multiple times a day. They are always the same, recalling his swift boat days patrolling the Mekong Delta. A few days later during an afternoon nap and during one of his dreams, he is awakened by the phone ringing. His doctor calls to inform him the tests reveal a tumor on his liver that needs to be biopsied as soon as possible. Chet realizes that his dreams are the result of PTSD and assumes his liver ailment must be a result of Agent Orange. He doesn't have the desire to seek treatment now after witnessing the effects of his wife's chemo and radiation treatment while she was being cared for at The Medical University of South Carolina.

Just thinking of a hospital takes away the good memories of him and Nancy having fun on weekends riding in horse and carriages, touring the historic city, and dining on low country cuisine. When Nancy was hospitalized in Charleston, he, his son, and daughter took eight hour shifts at the hospital towards the end of Nancy's life. The effects of suffering with cancer are embedded in Chet's mind, and there is no way he wants any part of chemotherapy.

As Chet continues to watch the sheer force of Hurricane Katrina and its flood surge on television, his dreams begin to bring him back to 1968. He reminisces about hearing strange gurgling sounds consistently calling for him. The sounds were very haunting, reminding him about the time his patrol boat was in the same area on The My Tho River on special missions. The gurgling sounds now come and go without any motive why. The small fishing village of Tra Vinh about 70 miles southwest of Saigon, now called Ho Chi Minh City, stays firmly in his mind night after night, and he starts realizing that the gurgling sounds must have had some sort of relevance. Trying to recall anything of importance after all these years, relating to the village of Tra Vinh is difficult. Replaying in his mind, Chet now realizes the gurgling sounds were the loudest while at the old marina area. Chet remembers even Buck acted startled and wouldn't stop barking when PCF-33 pulled into the old marina area. Rugby in a rare occasion had to hold back Buck with a leash. But, this all leads to some unanswered questions that need to be answered. What happened at the old marina? Why now is he being pulled back in time? Was there something his swift boat missed that day?

Chet concludes that the answers to his questions can only be found in Vietnam. Traveling half way around the world isn't something he wanted to do, but the force pulling him to get answers now begins to have priority. Taking into consideration his health status makes the decision much more complicated. Trying to jump each hurdle for taking the trip, Chet down plays his ailment and rises to the conclusion that there will be medical care available in Ho Chi Minh City if needed. Explaining to his family that he is visiting Vietnam because of hearing a gurgling sound wouldn't go very well, which forces him to tell them a little white lie. He comes up with the excuse of a Navy reunion for all crew members of PCF-33 in Old Saigon which seems to be well excepted by his son and daughter. After much thought, he decides to find out for himself and understands that looking for his answers may well have an unhappy ending. Using the internet, Chet finds various travel groups advertising tours of Vietnam and notices one offering the Mekong Delta area by riverboat. Thinking of himself as part of a travel group isn't something he's looking for. Knowingly Chet realizes that his travels need to take him wherever his inner thought directs him to go. Following the gurgling sounds in his mind, and his war memories make traveling with a tour group too restrictive and going solo makes more sense.

After thinking about the special relationship he once experienced with Buck, Chet decides not until he returns from his desired Vietnam trip will he consider owning his own chocolate lab. Waiting until he returns will provide him with the needed time to properly train his new dog without any distractions.

Chapter 2

2006 Kiawah Island, SC

Unknown forces acting like a well-made magnet and its strong magnetic force finally pull Chet to conclude he must go to Vietnam. In February after months of contemplation and procrastination, Chet finally takes the plunge and books his travel arrangements online. Flying out of Charleston, his travels will take him to San Francisco where he will stop for a few days to visit Big Sur, California. The beautiful town on the rocky shores of the Pacific Ocean, Big Sur is about a three-and-a-half-hour drive from the airport.

Big Sur was another favorite vacation destination for him and Nancy, especially when his west coast business travels allowed him to take some extra time off. The jagged cliffs pummeled by the Pacific surf line gave the town its famous natural attraction and is considered the most beautiful coast line in the world. Picturing himself and Nancy riding up and down the coast in their rented car (always the latest Mustang convertible, preferably red), Nancy's hair blowing in the wind, wearing a large brim straw hat with the biggest smile on her face. They would stop at certain points along the rocky coast and have a picnic while observing the masses of seal lounging on the rocks below. Occasionally they would view Humpback Whales in the distance soaring out of the water and while splashing back down into the deep blue sea.

Downshifting through the winding turns creates the perfect ingredient for reliving the route of their travels along the famous Highway 1. The beautiful surroundings generate the feel of Nancy's presence as Chet imagines her as his passenger. It brings back a familiar shiver of happiness as he wishes to go back in time for just one more day. Bringing back his traveling past gives him a special unforgettable feeling that he is once again as close as he can be to the love of his life, Nancy. Chet stays at the same romantic hotel as he did with Nancy, The Rocky Ranch Inn, which is situated on the cliffs of the Pacific Ocean. He books a modest room, feeling instead that the better rooms hanging over the cliffs with infinity pools would be too much to take due to the highly romantic settings and he being alone. Even the front desk clerk asks him at check-in if he will be alone and when he signals yes, the clerk shrugs her shoulders and gives the slightest sign of disbelief.

After the few days in Big Sur, Chet moved on to Honolulu for a short layover and then on to his destination, Ho Chi Minh City. The long flight takes a toll on Chet's body, but he is very happy that there wasn't any recurrent health issue. Once in Ho Chi Minh City, he registers at The Grand Hotel. During the registration process while waiting in line, Chet absorbs the hotel's elaborate décor. The lobby is lined with ebony wood panels and exotic hand-cut moldings that are all accented by black wrought iron gates and railings. Through Chet's eye's, the hotel has kept its regal elegance showing no signs of the war or any upheaval after the war.

After checking in and freshening up, he is ready to see Saigon again after almost forty years. Chet doesn't know what to expect as he begins his visit with an open mind. He first visits the old landmarks and is amazed at how much it has changed from the time in 1968 when he had taken a short leave from his Navy duties. The smells and fears of war are now gone, and Chet takes in the shear vitality of the city. He remembers the mass amounts of bicycles once filling the city streets. But now those bicycles are replaced with motorcycles and scooters. Gone are most of the rickshaws which carried merchant goods to and from markets leaving only an occasional rickshaw now used for tourist's purposes. Back in 1968, Chet remembers all government buildings were guarded by soldiers of the South Vietnamese Army while embassies saw army tanks surrounding their complexes. The new city now seems so much more at peace, and gone are all signs of the military using martial law.

While looking high above, Chet counts many building cranes in the process of erecting new high-rise offices and residences. Even the old parks in the center of the city have either been developed or completely remodeled. All the local citizens seem to be on their way to or from work as compared to what he remembers as the war-wounded were then begging in the streets. No longer any sign of orphan children asking for handouts while being chased by the military police. Chet stops and stares at the traffic roundabout of Nguyen Huu Canh at the foot of The Saigon River and gazes up river, witnessing one the most beautiful views of a city he has ever seen. He once stood in that same exact spot in 1968 as his memory flashes back the once ugly view against the new scenic view. This all made Chet feel as though there was still hope, and maybe some good came out of all the tragedies of war.

The next day, the morning dew droplets are feeding the hummingbird moths just outside his window, and Chet is amazed by their size and color. The first time he came across hummingbird moths was during the war along the banks of The My Tho River, their sheer vibrant primary colors stood out against the green backdrop of jungle vegetation. At the time, it made him wonder how the species could ever survive through all the bombings, napalm, and agent orange attacks.

By day three, the abdominal pains return, and Chet calls down to the front desk of the hotel and asks for the name of a doctor that he can call. They give him the name of a local doctor who will see him immediately. Dr. Diem is a strange bird whose office is down the street from The Grand hotel. Chet climbs a long flight of stairs and enters the doctor's office with his stomach pain now throbbing. Dr. Diem's office is like stepping back in time with extremely high ceilings and very large windows overlooking the main street below. Chet's eyes roam the large room, noticing an abundance of Vietnamese "Hoi An Silk Lanterns" and bamboo partitions. The room appearance gives Chet the impression that back in the day this space might have been some sort of restaurant. The walls are lined with pictures taken well over thirty years ago, and the doctor is in most of the pictures wearing a North Vietnamese Army uniform. Chet wants no part of this and when he is just about to walk out, Dr. Diem enters the room speaking English, asking him his symptoms. The doctor stares out the large window while Chet explains his ills. The doctor's only treatment is to begin Chet on holistic herbs. The doctor suggests Chet immediately begin drinking the locally made tonic consisting of certain roots, berries, and who knows what else. It smells and tastes like crap, and although he thinks Dr. Diem is crazy, Chet has no other choice but to comply. Never once does Chet mention his diagnosed disorder with the doctor. Dr. Diem doesn't even use a stethoscope or check Chet's abdominal area for lumps and bulges. Dr. Diem provides Chet with directions to drink an ounce of the tonic every six hours, stay in his room, and call him in 48 hours to advise how he is doing. Chet's not happy that he must be constrained to his small room for two whole days.

After twenty-four hours, Chet's pain eases showing small signs of remission. Being cooped up seems to instigate his memory and again, he begins to hear the exact same gurgling sound that he heard over thirty-eight years ago. The gurgling sounds are now at half hour intervals making him feel even more curious than ever. All these odd feelings start to take effect on Chet's emotions and wonders why he keeps hearing those sounds. He questions his being in Vietnam in the first place and now considers it a dumb idea. Wanting to just have a conversation with anyone seems like a good idea, and he figures the hotel bar would be a great place to go.

Chet makes his way downstairs and walks into a room that has a wonderful old hand-carved bar that seems to have survived the war years. The bartender walks toward him, and Chet orders a Chardonnay with Campari thinking that it may help settle his sour stomach. After ten minutes or so, Chet notices the person sitting two seats away. A well-spoken Vietnamese silver-haired middle-aged man having a discussion with the bartender in English. As the bartender's talking, he seems to pause when a waiter approaches the bar to have an order filled. Chet strikes up a conversation by introducing himself and the silver-haired man introduces himself as Ta Ning who happens to be from Tra Vinh. Chet explains that he spent some time stopping in Tra Vinh during his Navy swift boat days. Ta recalls his childhood and remembers the Navy swift boats as a young boy during the war sometimes using the village as a short resting point. The two talk about politics and world affairs. After an hour of discussion, both feel that the United States pulling out of Vietnam in 1973 was a big mistake causing the annihilation of hundreds of thousands of innocent people. During these conversations with Ta, Chet's gurgling sounds radiate to a new level, almost as though it was coming from within the bar area.

Ta also admits if it were not for America's role in the war, many more of his people would have been killed by the Viet Cong long before the withdrawal. Chet determines that Ta was about thirteen or fourteen years old back in 1968 and now looks ten years older than he is. Ta Ning explains that his mother and father were killed by the Viet Cong in 1966 and kidnapped his sister, never to be seen again. Ta explained that he and the other children of the village had to beg, borrow, and steal to stay alive. Ta goes into a very detailed description of the atrocities he witnessed as a young boy. Ta clearly describes what would happen if a single family member was suspected of helping U.S. forces; the entire family would be executed. Mass graves would be dug by local villagers at gun point, then they would be shot in place, falling into their own graves. He explains that he and his friends would steal anything given the chance from the Viet Cong, even though it was risky. They clearly knew that if they ever got caught, the Viet Cong would kill them in an instant and hang them publicly for all the other villagers to see.

Chet makes the remark to Ta that the war would not have lasted if it wasn't for the dumb Rules of Engagement in effect. He explains that commanding a swift boat had three main rules to follow.

> Rule #1-Direct fire against any suspected enemy activity was prohibited unless the U.S. vessel had first received incoming fire from the suspected activity.

> Rule #2-Indirect fire in support of land units required that the firing vessel obtain previous authorization involved co-operation between the U.S. Navy and U.S. Army commands. This usually took several hours. By the time the permission arrived, the need for indirect fire support had long since pasted.

> Rule #3-Swift boats were specifically restricted from operating inside rivers in areas beyond just the immediate sea entrance.

Chet goes on to say that night time patrolling was infrequent, but when used, it increased the danger factor by ten. On a certain night in August 1968, he enlightens Ta with a story of the most dangerous patrol which took his swift boat so far up the river they ended up running aground right in the middle of a rice paddy. With the engines stuck in mud, the entire crew then jumped during the black of night into the shallow water to try and wiggle the boat into deeper water. The soft muddy bottom under their boots didn't help at all to give them any traction to move. Their shear manpower was not enough to budge the boat even an inch. They were now sitting ducks for the Viet Cong to come and attack. Using any lights on board, making sounds, or using their radio was out of the question since it would give away their position to the enemy. Chet, along with all the other crew members, felt as though that was the day they would meet their divine maker. All they could do was to hope the Viet Cong didn't notice them and patiently wait for the lift of the next high tide before sunrise. In the meantime, Buck proudly stood his watch alongside the crew while silently giving Rugby signals of any unknown movement or scents. Chet knew that it was a good time to pray to himself and felt his buddies were doing the same.

After a few hours, the crew started hearing a mild screeching sound of the hull which confirms their hope that the high tide is moving in, and freeing themselves was within reach. Just as the black of night turns into dark gray, the hull lifts enough to start floating once again. All hands jump back into the shallow water to turn the boat around while walking it into deeper waters so the engines can be started, and they could race their way out to safety.

Once back at the swift boat command, boat Lieutenant Horner had some serious explaining to do. Running aground in the Navy is never considered a good thing, but under the circumstances of ordering such a high-risk mission in a hot hostile area in the dead of night brought no reprimand. After Lt. Horner was finished with his informal investigation, he summoned the crew to an empty supply storage building. Chet and his crew members wondered what the Lieutenant had in mind. When the Lieutenant walked into the building holding something wrapped in cloth under his arm, attention on deck was called. Very slowly Lieutenant Horner unwrapped the cloth, exposing a bottle of Jack Daniels and six small shot glasses. Each of the crew members made a toast as the Lieutenant thanked all for a job well done. That day's events all summed up to just another unusual day in the brown water Navy.

A dangerous river with the beautiful name of "Perfume River" was filled with Viet Cong. The river got its name during the autumn season, when up-river thousands upon thousands of fallen orchards would float in the water, giving the river a perfume-like aroma, hence the nickname. Two weeks after running a ground while at the mouth of the Perfume River, the swift boat crew was spraying agent orange onto the river banks to emulsify all vegetation. Suddenly Chet receives a sniper fire bullet fragment in his left thigh. The bullet ricochets off a wrench and at first Chet is unaware he is hit until he starts to feel his left leg warm and wet with blood. The wound is severe enough to cause massive bleeding and tourniquet is set around his leg. PCF-33 rushes back to base where he is transferred and flown by chopper to "The Heilen," a German passenger ship that had been converted into a floating hospital to treat mostly civilian casualties. Due to the height of "The Tet Offensive" taking place, all other ships are filled with the wounded. Chet describes his recovery on "The Heilen" as intense while receiving the highest nursing care one could receive by American Red Cross staffing. His recovery takes less time than the doctors originally predicted, and Chet attributes the Red Cross nursing staff the reason. He is again ready for duty and back on PCF-33 in four weeks.

Chet and Ta's discussion continued into the wee hours of the morning, so they exchanged cell phone numbers and instantly became friends which gave Chet a strong feeling of trust. The next day, Chet decides to call Ta and ask him if he would be interested in tagging along on the way to Tra Vinh. Ta agrees and says it's the least I could do for someone who gave Vietnam so much. They both plan to leave from Ho Chi Minh City in Chet's rental smart car the very next morning. The car is so small that Chet's almost 230 pounds filled up a seat and a half by himself while the temperature is about 98 degrees, and it's still only morning. Along the very hot and uncomfortable ride, Ta seems a little edgy, and Chet asks if there is something wrong, but a nod of his head indicates a no answer.

As they near their destination, Ta is silently carrying a haunting burden on his shoulders as he brings up the Typhoon of 1968. The historical storm hit the village of Tra Vinh real hard causing a flooding surge of at least fifteen feet. He explains the effects of the storm wiped out most of the village and the countless amounts of dead bodies floated up and down the river. The land was so flooded that burial was almost impossible to accomplish for those who didn't survive. Chet also recalled the smells of death when his swift boat first arrived in Tra Vinh three or four days after the storm, and he compares what he hears from Ta to what he had watched during the television coverage of Hurricane Katrina.

Chapter 3

1966 Saigon, South Vietnam

The times are once again swiftly changing right before his very eyes. There is nothing he can do but forcibly watch with wide open eyes as a knife is held firmly against his throat. There are six vicious men who have chased down his family's whereabouts finding them in a small house in the countryside just south of Saigon. He is only a boy of eleven-years-old when his life is suddenly torn apart. None of this makes sense to him as he tries to question the religious motives in his mind.

His beautiful mother, Kim, was slim and resembled a China porcelain faced doll with long, black, silky hair down to her knees. His father, Ho, had a small build and was always full of energy. He always considered his father more intelligent than most well-educated men. His strong knit family kept him sheltered up to this point in his life, displaying nothing but love for him and his six-year-old younger sister. The young boy is now filled with terror, and he begins to pray for his family's safety.

The six men are Viet Cong, and they want the boy to witness the execution of his mother and father knowing that it will send a strong message to the others who are resisting the communist forces from the north. The boy painfully watches his younger sister, Khanh, ripped apart from his mother and taken away crying and screaming, never to be seen again. Both parents are gagged and tied up at gun point leaving them totally helpless as they watch their nightmare develop into true horror.

The young boy, Ta, only last week sensed something was wrong, asking his father what was going on and why were they planning to move once again. He was told by his father a story only seven days ago that made no sense to him then. Ta watched many nearby families pack and leave their homes, carrying on their backs their most prized possessions. Ta now questions if he should have paid more attention to what his father was saying as today he is forced to begin to fill in the many empty pieces to a puzzle himself.

Trying hard not to focus on the horrific view of his parents at gun point, Ta begins to concentrate on recalling his father's words. Slowly Ta drifts into the summer of 1954 when after seventy years of rule, the French finally admit their losses and abruptly leave Vietnam creating a large vacuum for power and control. The streets of Hanoi were packed with people lighting off firecrackers and proudly waving the new Vietnamese flag. All signs, billboards, and display windows showing any French connection were quickly taken down, fiercely broken into pieces and set on fire. Vast amounts of everyday people formed into large crowds parading and chanting "Freedom at last" up and down the main streets of Hanoi. Nothing but renewed optimism and joy were being expressed by the people who now looked forward to a new life and government.

The country was unfortunately already divided into two sections, the north favoring a new communist government and the south wanting to be a democracy. The true hope of the new established country was to somehow find a common link and unite as one. Ho was then the postmaster of Hanoi and for the first time, he saw that his country was at the brink of a new age without any foreign influence for the first time.

Filled with optimism, Ho and his newly wed wife, Kim, shortly decided to start a family, and their first born was a boy they named Ta. It was the late fall of 1955 and things were looking up, except for political rumbling which Ho and Kim tried to pay no attention to. The family had more than most with Ho working for the government as it gave them job security, or so they thought. The political forces began to take root and slowly before their eyes, Ho and Kim watched a more stringent form of government take over everyday liberties by restricting what they can say and do. The young couple, along with their son Ta, stood fast on their beliefs, thinking that if they stayed out of what was going on politicly throughout the country, their home would remain a safe place.

By 1960 Ho and Kim had a daughter they named Khanh just when the tides of change suddenly shifted North Vietnam into a state of repression. The boarder of the now separated north and south was firmly set. Fighting began to be an everyday occurrence with civil war becoming the new talk of the day. Rumors of mass assassinations and kidnapping began to become a reality, and those same sophisticated people who once celebrated the end of French rule now wished the French would have never left.

In 1964 still being the postmaster, Ho noticed that too many of his postal customers were being swept up by the government never to be seen again. Fellow Catholic friends of Ho tried to convince him that most of the government sweeps were ordered to eliminate Catholics who were an unwanted minority. Gradually one by one, Ho lost his Catholic friends and family either by government sweeps or them moving south to more friendly grounds. It wasn't until 1966 that Ho realized he must leave Hanoi and take his family south.

After a restless night in the spring of 1966, Ho and his family abruptly became refugees within the very same country they loved so much. Ho questions why he and his family stayed in the north this long, hoping now that it was not too late to seek safety in the south.

The family packed up their most treasured possessions and began their trip on foot to Saigon, hoping not to be stopped by government police or soldiers along the way. On their travels to the south, Ta remembers him and his family on many occasions hiding from soldiers and trying to only move during twilight or dawn hours so as not to be noticed. Even though he knew what could happen to him and his family, Ho decided not to display any signs of fear regarding the real dangers if they happened to be stopped along the way.

Due to their limited traveling time window (twilight and dawn), the family didn't arrive in Saigon until two weeks later. Walking and hitching rides wherever possible, the family learned to make the best of whatever was available to them even if it meant using a secret underground movement of Catholic volunteers who sheltered them during their southbound trip.

Ho and his family settled in a countryside town called An Phuoc just east of Saigon where he rented a small home. Finding work was not easy due to the flood of refugees from the north. Ho was lucky enough to find employment at a laundry. He was very happy just to find any work in order for him to put food on the table for his family. Never once did Ho think hard work in 100+ degree temperatures were beneath him or his abilities. He felt very thankful to the same underground group for finding him a job.

The loud sounds of POP! POP! suddenly awake Ta from his dream, and his eyes refocus on his parents now laying on the floor with blood spouting from their bruised and beaten heads. The two sharp sounds were rifle shots into the temples of his mother and father. Ta stares at his parent's inert bodies hoping for them to show the slightest movement or a sign of life. All he saw were the two lifeless bodies of his mother and father. For the first time in his life, Ta breaks down in uncontrollable tears, freezing the site of his dead parents into his mind to never be forgotten. Ta's immediate mental attention is drawn to nothing but taking revenge when and if the opportunity arises. Boiling anger takes control of his inner spirit, and he quickly sheds his boyish demeanor, hurriedly becoming a man. Ta promises himself that he will do what it takes to have the evil Viet Cong pay the price for killing his family.

Ta is then dragged out of the house feet first and roughed up and beaten by the Viet Cong. They take him to an unknown location where he is set free to send a message to the other orphans who have been creating havoc by stealing food and setting off booby traps which are meant for U.S. armed forces. The warning given to Ta to pass on to the other orphans was, "Sure death to all" if they continue their antics.

The next few years of living off the land by stealing food and supplies from the Viet Cong have become routine and, in fact, quite enjoyable for Ta. He realizes that in a small way this was only the beginning of obtaining his revenge. A few big troubling thoughts remained on his mind every day of his life for which he always tried to find closure, but never did. The first was the fact that he was never able to find out what happened to his sister, Khanh, left only to assume she was enslaved by the Viet Cong and became another victim succumbing to a tragic ending. Secondly, Ta's parents' bodies were dumped in an unknown location which eluded Ta's mission in life to find out where they were. Ta always felt a large empty void in his life for not knowing the final fate of his family members remains. Ta takes an oath and swears to himself that he will dedicate his life to insuring that no surviving relative ever experience such a devastating loss.

Chapter 4

1964 Quincy, Illinois

Blurring images of fertile prime farmland whisking by, Mia Flynn is almost hypnotized from her window seat of a Greyhound Bus. Leaving her hometown of Quincy, IL and all the memories of her past, Mia has decided to carve out a new future. Her destination is the midsized college of Southern Illinois University located in Carbondale, IL and its highly-regarded nursing program.

The city of Quincy is just across the river from Hannibal, MO, the birthplace of Samuel Langhorne Clemens who used the pen name of Mark Twain. Local children in the Quincy public school system quickly learn at an early age of their famous hometown author. All the classic stories of the famous American writer were based on the life and detailed living conditions along the Mississippi River basin. Quincy's nickname is the "Gem City," and during the 19th Century it was a thriving transportation center as riverboats and rail service linked the city to many key destinations along the river. In 1870, it was once Illinois's second largest city.

As a young girl, Mia remembers playing with friends in the caves along the banks of the Mississippi and its legendary history. Her and her friends would play a game called "Huck Finn" which was a form of "Hide and Seek," but the person who had to find others was called a vagabond. Each spring during heavy rainfall, Quincy residences pray the flooding Mississippi doesn't reach its warning markers which are attached onto river navigation signs. History has shown many times dangerous flood waters had reached twenty feet above flood stage.

Mia was an only child and orphaned at the young age of eleven. Her parents were killed in a snow storm related auto accident trying to get back to Quincy after her paternal grandmother's death. Mia grew up with her maternal grandmother, Grammy, who gave never-ending love and care in place of her parents, but was 65 years of age at the time and had a failing health condition. Growing up with Grammy placed Mia in a peculiar situation, especially when Grammy had to visit school. All her friends thought she was her mother, and they made fun of her. Mia was too embarrassed to tell her friends the truth about being an orphan, so she learned to live with it.

Trying to fulfill her dream of becoming a nurse, Mia attended Vatterott College located in Quincy for her two-year program certificate. After graduation she planned to transfer to a four-year college for her final nursing degree. Throughout her last year at Vatterott College, Grammy's health is failing while Mia tries balancing her life as a caretaker and full-time student at the same time. During her last month at Vatterott College, she is called to come down to the student record office just as she arrives at her second class of the day. Mia arrives at the student records office feeling worrisome and hopes that she will not be given any bad news about Grammy. When Mia arrives, she is asked to be seated in the school administrator's office. She is sadly informed of Grammy's death which she saw coming in the distant future, but not this soon. Mia now realizes that there was no one left in her life to lean on. The timing of Grammy's passing is very hard for Mia to accept, especially when it was so close to her next college planning stage. She's now totally on her own and with Grammy's death, now loses the last living connection with her deceased parents.

Surviving on her own, she reaches the age of twenty years old with two years of nursing courses under her belt. Being able to squeeze in a full-time job and school is challenging, but her schedule is flexible enough to do both. Mia's parents left her a one hundred-thousand-dollar insurance policy which Grammy was smart enough to place in a trust for Mia. Between her working income and trust fund, she has enough to pay for all college costs and have money left over to save for the future. Attending an in-state university like SIU also gives her residency discounts. Mia now must start thinking about her future and making her dreams of a nursing career come to life.

Parting from "Packer Land" isn't an easy thing to do. The northeastern section of Wisconsin in and around the Green Bay area proudly carries the name of "Packer Land" in honor of their famous football team and coach. The famous head coach named Vince Lombardi grew up in Brooklyn, NY and graduated from Fordham University in 1937. By 1947 he was offered an assistant coaching position at his alma mater for basketball and football. Following in 1948, Lombardi was accepted as an assistant coaching position at the United States Military Academy in West Point, NY. In 1954 Lombardi at the age of 41, became the offensive coordinator for the New York Giants Football team, and worked his way up to assistant coach. For the 1958 NFL season, the Packers, with five future hall of famers playing on the team, finished with a record of 1 win, 10 loses and 1 tie. The Packer shareholders were disheartened and the Green Bay community was enraged. The financial viability, and the very existence of the Green Bay Packers franchise were in jeopardy. On February 2, 1959, Vince Lombardi accepted the position of head coach and general manager of the Green Bay Packers. The combination of focusing on the undiscovered talent and hard workout routines helped create one of professional sports strongest dynasty's.

A twenty-year-old named Jill Landry is saying goodbye to her mom, Edith, father, Dave, and sister, Ali, who is two years younger. The town is Peshtigo, WI, and the Landry family along with the entire population of the town are avid Green Bay Packer fans. Jill's favorite player is Paul Hornung whose nickname is the "Golden Boy," and he is the first NFL player to win the Heisman Trophy. The town of Peshtigo has a strange infamous history. Back on October 8, 1871, a forest fire driven by strong winds totally consumed the town along with a dozen other villages, killing over two thousand people. The fire, known as the Peshtigo Fire, is the deadliest in American history. Unidentifiable remains of hundreds of residents were buried in a mass grave at the Peshtigo Fire Cemetery. On the same day in 1871, there were four other major fires located in Chicago, Illinois, Holland, Port Huron, and Manistee, Michigan. History now only remembers the great Chicago fire.

By 1963 Green Bay's head coach Vince Lombardi is considered a god and running back Paul Hornung, along with quarterback Bart Starr are idols. The team is credited with two winning Super Bowls 1 and 11, five NFL championships in-1961, 1962, 1965, 1966, and 1967.

Trying to make up for the lost time saying goodbye to her family, Jilly needs to rush her driving to make up the lost hour back in Peshtigo. To help pass the hours, she brought her portable cassette player and a shoebox filled with tapes. Attempting to get the best quality of sound while also stopping the player from falling off the seat, she places it under the driver's seat. The sound improves, and the tape player is finally in a secured place if she hit the brakes. Listening to the upbeat tempos of The Four Tops, The Supremes, and The Temptations stimulates her inner rhythms by having her forget how fast she is traveling. With her head shaking side to side to the beat of the music, she gives a quick peek at her rearview mirror. In the far distance, Jilly sees a flashing blue light moving at a rapid speed toward her. Within thirty seconds the flashing blue lights are in her face, and she panics. Not knowing what to do, the flashing lights move to the right lane, and she notices a police officer pointing her to pull over. Jilly has never been given any type of traffic violation before, and her heart begins to beat at a faster rate.

Pulling over to the right-hand shoulder, and coming to a full stop seems like an eternity. The police car parks right behind her and with its lights still flashing, the trooper steps out and walks toward Jilly's car. Jilly quickly turns off the tape player. She reads the markings on the car as "Illinois State Police" and fears the worst will happen. She is asked where is she headed, and she replies SIU in Carbondale. "What's your major?" asked the trooper. "Nursing," replied Jilly. She was then asked to hand over her driver's license and vehicle registration which she complied with. The trooper took her documents and walked back to his car and sat back in his seat. Five minutes later the trooper returns and hands her a ticket. She looks at the ticket, and the trooper remarks that it's only for going eight miles an hour over the posted speed limit. He informs her that she was moving twenty over the posted speed limit, and a ticket for such a severe speed would require a court appearance. The trooper has Jilly promise that she will watch her speed in the future and if he catches her again, he'll press for the limits.

From the time she was a teenager, Jilly had the desire to become a registered nurse. It's now the only goal in her life that means something to her. Deciding to transfer from Berlin College in Green Bay, WI to Southern Illinois University was an emotional decision. Her parents, Edith and Dave, are not happy about her living away from home and worry about her safety. Jilly wants to learn more about the world, but keeps her future wishes from her parents. Knowing that if she brought it up in conversation, her dad would probably explode.

Mia observes the confusion of new students walking around the college campus as though they were tourists. A flyer handout was given to all newbies with a map of the campus announcing a meeting. The two girls almost walk into each other while entering the school's performing arts center. The get acquainted gathering in the PAC is already filled. Mia is circling the room, trying hard to find a seat. Not paying attention she, again, bumps into Jilly. They make eye contact and give each other a cracked smile as they decide to sit on the floor against a wall next to each other.

The school introduction meeting goes well. Mia is attracted to Jilly writing franticly as though she was taking minutes of the meeting. Mia wonders what the heck could she be writing? After all was said by the administrators, a motion to adjoin was called and seconded. Mia takes one last glance at Jilly, still writing away. A crowd is now trying to exit using the same walled aisle. Mia places her hand on Jilly's shoulder and gives a little shake so she doesn't get stepped on.

Most of the newbies head for the cafeteria after the meeting and both Mia and Jilly, who are starving, are no exception. With a capacity crowd, both girls standing nowhere near each other find themselves waiting for a seat to open. Suddenly in the middle of the cafeteria, a double seat becomes vacant. Jilly swiftly walks toward the table, arrives at one of the empty seats, and notices Mia swinging in to the other. The first to break the ice is Mia who introduces herself and holds out her right hand to shake Jilly's hand.

Both bring up their backgrounds and how badly each wants to become a nurse. Their conversation becomes centered on nursing. As their dinner gets cold, each explains their dreams of why they want to become a nurse. Mia suggests that since they have so much in common, why don't they become roommates. Mia asks, "What was all the writing about in the PAC?" Jilly tells her that she was writing a letter to her mom explaining that she was happy to be away from home and not to worry. Mia responded, "It must be nice to have a mom to lean on."

Early the next morning, Mia hands in a request to change her roommate, which is approved, giving the two young women a better chance to grow closer. While unpacking their things, the two discover another common thread of friendship. Their birthdays are only a day apart, Mia on March 5th and Jilly, March 6th, born the same year of 1944. Jilly feels awful about Mia not having any living family and for the first time, silently accepts her as her own sister. They declare a pact to remain buddies to the end, at least until graduation, regardless of the many unknown influences which lie ahead.

Settling into their normal daily college routine finds the girls sharing many of the same classes. A few weeks later, both girls overhear some classmates mentioning that this Sunday night, February 9th, The Ed Sullivan Show was going to have as guests The Beatles. Jilly and Mia were so caught up in their college entry, they completely missed all the media hype and are thrilled that they will get the chance view the show. They can't wait to witness television history, and Jilly suggests they both drive to Peshtigo that weekend and stay over at her parents' place. Realizing that she will get to spend real family time, longing for some sort of bond, Mia is anxious to meet Edith, Dave, and Ali. They didn't have to be back in class until Tuesday which gives them a nice long weekend to spend together.

The 570 mile drive to Peshtigo begins very early in the morning. Only twenty miles out of Carbondale, Mia, who is driving, decides to make a quick detour through Quincy. Her intentions are to show Jilly where she grew up with her grammy and where she lived as a child. Passing along the small towns along the Mississippi River, Mia begins to reminisce the old days when she lived with her parents. Her former red brick elementary school has been closed and now has been converted into an office building. The open fields that she played in as a young girl are now a strip mall and parking lot. When they arrive at Grammy's old house, Jilly notices that a large "For Sale" sign posted on the front lawn showing that it's an estate sale. Mia explains that a local attorney is handling her grammy's estate which primarily is only the house, and she hopes the home will sell soon.

Driving through the town of Peshtigo while Jilly is showing off her old schools and playing places, Mia notices all the "Go Packers" signs still on front lawns almost covered in snow. Jilly yelps out, "Welcome to Packer land." Passing the local Kroger Supermarket, Mia notices an outdoor thermometer reading -4 degrees. The coldest temperature she ever saw was last year at -26 degrees.

At last they reach 106 Eagle Street, and Jilly makes a left turn into the driveway. The sound of crackling snow under the wheels of the car attracts someone inside the house to peek through the bay window venetian blinds. Wearing only pink polka dot pajamas, Jilly's sister, Ali, runs out the front door to greet the arriving college students. Mia is given a big hug by Ali and observes that the freezing temperature has no effect on her. Ali grabs the two small overnight bags in the trunk and runs into the house yelling, "They're here, Mom!"

Meeting Edith for the first time brings Mia back to an old familiar place that she hasn't seen or felt in many years. Edith is wearing a floral print house dress and a contrasting black and white stripe apron. Wiping her hands, she walks toward Mia with open arms giving her a holding hug only a mother would give. Unknown to Mia, Edith received a call from Jilly a few days before detailing Mia's loss of her family. Without showing any sentiments, Edith is hurting inside just thinking about Mia's loss. The hug is so memorable it stimulates Mia's emotions as Edith's facial features mold into her own mother's. Mia is taken back by the illusion as she is caught with a bewildered expression on her face by Jilly.

Paying no attention to his surroundings, Dave is carrying on about a replay of the 1963 NFL Championship game. Mia reaches out to shake his hand as Jilly introduces her friend Mia. Dave askes, "Isn't Mia the name of that actress in that new television show, Peyton Place?" Ali responds, "Yes, Dad, you mean Mia Farrow." Edith offers Mia a drink of warm apple cider, and they all gather in the living room to settle in before dinner. Ali recites the dinner menu to Jilly and Mia as cucumber salad, pot roast, braised onions, mashed potatoes, and pecan pie for dessert. Finishing dinner with many hours of traveling behind them, Mia and Jilly are exhausted. They both decide to go to bed early. Getting a good night sleep will rekindle all their excitement in the morning.

Early Sunday morning before the sun was up, Mia smelled something very familiar. Putting her robe on, she walked out of the guest room and down the hallway. Just before reaching the kitchen, she heard the crackling sound of bacon and the smell of baked cinnamon buns in the oven. Remembering her mom making a full breakfast on Sunday mornings brings a tear to her eyes. A loud sounding, "Good morning, Mia" from Edith snaps her from the trance. Jilly then enters the kitchen, and Edith reminds them that it's Sunday, and we are all going to church after breakfast.

After church Mia tells Ali and Jilly that she is glad she came to visit their home and feels as though she is part of the family. Ali and Jilly already feel the same and both tell Mia that they will accept her as a sister. Edith overhears them, standing by the doorway, and walks to Mia for another motherly hug.

All four women join in hugging as Edith says she is now the proud mother of three daughters.

Sunday afternoon actions bring the three girls to French Street Pond where Jilly and Ali promised to teach Mia to ice skate. Mia borrows an extra pair of ice skates from Ali, and Jilly packs an old kitchen chair in the trunk of her car. Mia questions taking the chair, and the only explanation from Jilly is, "You'll see." The chair is placed on the ice, and Jilly shows how to hold on while moving her skates effortlessly across the ice. Mia picks up on using the chair as a tool and starts to move her skates and begins to glide around the frozen pond.

In the back of Mia's mind, she remembers as a young girl when her father tried teaching her to ice skate. It was right after Christmas in 1953, and she had been given a pair of ice skates from her parents. Mia had a very difficult time keeping her balance. After a half hour of trying, she fell hard on her left elbow and dislocated her shoulder. Abruptly that happy day turned into a not so happy day; Mia had to be rushed to a hospital. It was Mia's first time in a hospital, and she never forgot the caring nurse who treated her in the emergency room. Being frightened with her shoulder filled with pain, the nurse made it a point to first settle Mia down. Then in a soft soothing voice, she explained what she was going to do. Mia still remembers that composure making her pain go away. That nurse set a high standard in Mia's mind for her to meet in life and helped her choose nursing as a career.

Dave already decided not to view The Ed Sullivan show and that he will make up an excuse about having paperwork due on Monday for work. He isn't happy about the long-haired singing wonders anyway. The four women will tune into CBS along with 73 million other viewers that evening, making it one of the seminal moments ever on television.

Longer than anyone wanted to wait, it was finally Sunday at 8 pm. Gathering around the "black and white" Admiral television was Jilly, Mia, Ali, and Edith. Dave made it clear that he had no desire to watch four mop heads, as he put it, sing silly songs. The anticipation and excitement between the three girls starts to brush against Edith causing her to show a slight eagerness herself. Mia, Jilly, and Ali sit within three feet, right in front of the 14" television screen, and Mia leans over to Jilly and makes the comment that it's only 77 days since President Kennedy was assassinated, and Jill responds with a sad frown.

Ed Sullivan opened the show by briefly mentioning a congratulatory telegram to The Beatles from Elvis and his manager, Colonel Tom Parker, and then hurriedly to advertisements for Aero Shave and Griffin Shoe Polish. The girls can't believe commercials playing so soon, and each of them let out big groans. Jilly starts to hug Mia. They are both shaking like a leaf with excitement and turn their heads toward the television absorbing each word said. After the commercial break, Ed made his memorable introduction:

"Now yesterday and today, our theater's been jammed with newspapermen and hundreds of photographers from all over the nation, and these veterans agreed with me that this city never has witnessed the excitement stirred by these youngsters from Liverpool who call themselves The Beatles. Now tonight you're going to be entertained twice by them. Right now and again in the second half of our show."

Happy tears begin to run down Mia and Jilly's cheeks as Ed Sullivan says, "Ladies and gentlemen, The Beatles! Let's bring them on."

At last John, Paul, George, and Ringo came onto the stage opening with "All My Loving" evoking ear-splitting screeches from teenaged girls in the audience. The Beatles followed that hit with Paul McCartney taking the spotlight to sing "Till There Was You." Mia now totally falls in love with George. During the song, a camera cut to each member of the band and introduced them to the audience by displaying their first name on screen. Jilly now declares she is also in love with Paul. When the camera cut to John Lennon, the caption below his name also read "SORRY GIRLS, HE'S MARRIED." The Beatles wrapped up the first set with "She Loves You," and the show went to a commercial again resulting in more moans and groans by the three girls.

Upon return from commercial, magician Fred Kaps took the stage to perform a set of sleight-of-hand tricks. As it turns out, Fred Kaps was a world renown magician, but he had bad luck on this day in 1964 to be the act that followed the Beatles. At this point, both women couldn't stop talking about what they just witnessed. Mia couldn't stop talking about George, but Jilly was contradicting her saying Paul was best by far. Ali thought John was cute and had the best head of hair. From that moment on, the music became embedded in their minds and was forever an important part of their everyday lives.

The panicked shaking of all three girls just gets worse as the second half of the show begins. The Beatles begin singing "I Saw Her Standing There" and "I Want to Hold Your Hand" to the delight of Mia, Jilly, and Ali. Each one again declares who their favorite Beatle is with Mia again claiming George, Jilly still dreams of Paul, while Ali clutches on for John. Jilly reminds her sister that John is married, and Ali gives a big sigh and says, "That's not fair. I'm now stuck with Ringo." Edith remarks, "I think all four Beatles are cute."

That night the girls barely slept, talking about their idols into the wee hours of the morning. Mia finally tells Jilly and Ali the real reason she likes George Harrison the best. She explains what happened to her in the summer of 1963 when she and Grammy visited her great aunt who lived in Benton, IL. Mia's great aunt's neighbor is George Harrison's real-life sister, Louise. George's sister lives in Benton with her husband, Gordon, their children, and a German Shepard named Sheba. George and his brother Peter came to visit their older sister that summer. Mia then tells them, "I had the honor of meeting both George and Peter." At the time, Mia didn't know who George Harrison was and for that matter, had never even heard of the Beatles. Mia sensed something special about George and his funny accent as he told her of his traveling around Europe and performing to sellout crowds. Mia goes on further to say, "George even invited me to tag along with the family so he could shop for records." Mia tells Jilly and Ali that while on their shopping trip, "George lost his wallet which was finally found by a local teenage boy and returned." Mia explains that she just so happened to be carrying her camera with her and took a picture of George and his family in front of the record store. After shopping they all stopped at the A&W Root Beer Restaurant on Route 37. It was quite obvious that George couldn't help but gawk at the waitresses who were wearing short-shorts as they served customers on roller skates. Mia then reaches into her handbag and takes out the photo she took in Benton. Ali quickly grabs the picture from Mia's hand, looks at it and yells, "Oh my god!" Jilly takes the photo from Ali and gives it a look and says, "Wow, Mia, you never mentioned this before." Mia tells Jilly, "I was holding off until the right time."

Mia and Jilly had such a good time in Peshtigo they both decide to make the trek every chance they get whenever a long weekend became available. Mia now considers Jilly and Ali as her newly acquired sisters. Mia asks Edith if it's okay to call her Mom instead of Edith. Hearing Edith's response of yes gives her chills, and she is now as happy as a fly on honey and feels a void in her life has been filled.

Chapter 5

1966 Carbondale, Illinois

Strings of colored lights, decorated trees, and even Santa himself are beginning to come down and stored away for another year. January is a month to rest and recuperate with all the holidays finally coming to an end. Mia and Jilly begin to make many new friends and are invited to a party at a nearby fraternity this upcoming Saturday night. At first they didn't want to go until other nursing students guaranteed them that Beatles music would be played. It was no secret in their dormitory that Mia and Jill's favorite music was anything by The Beatles. The girls often kept their door open during the day while they played the music loudly with most other residents singing along.

In Jilly's car on their way to East Grand Avenue fraternity house, Mia turns on the radio and scans the channels, stopping on a local station. The next song was introduced by the nighttime disk jockey as something new by The Beatles. Jilly shouts out loud, "Oh my God, can't believe it!" Mia begins to jump up and down in her seat as Jilly pulls over to the curb.

The new song was introduced as "In My Life" with mythical words flowing out of the harmonizing singers John, Paul, and George. When the song was over, Jilly and Mia sat motionless for many minutes without saying a word. The song's impression was like sending an arrow through their hearts. Mia began to cry like a baby, and Jilly shortly joined in. They both then knew this was the one song that had an everlasting emotional effect on each of them. Jilly wanted the song to be a testimonial to their deep friendship, and Mia totally agreed.

After arriving at the fraternity party, Mia and Jilly decide to stay together and be sort of wallflowers while just enjoying the music, but it didn't last very long. A good-looking young man walked over to Mia and said, "Hi, my name is John Ricciardi, but my friends call me Ricky. What's your name?"

Mia paid no attention to him and finally said, "I'm here with my friend Jilly just to enjoy the music."

Ricky said "Great! I have a friend standing over there named George Wilkerson who is too embarrassed to talk to strange girls." Both Jilly and Mia looked over to see who Ricky was pointing at. Ricky asked them if he could have his friend come over and join their conversation. Mia at that moment looks at Jilly, and she gives a nod of approval. Mia asked why he was called Ricky when his name was John? Ricky describes when he was in elementary school, his friends kept thinking his last name was Riccardo just like Ricky Ricardo on the TV show "I Love Lucy." The nickname stuck and ever since then, even his family members called him Ricky.

It turned out that George is a great joke teller; he loved the classic humor of Henny Youngman, the new rising stars Rodney Dangerfield, and George Carlin. Within a short period of time, he had the group laughing so loudly that other party goers began to give them weird looks. The laughter was so intense that it began to hurt the girls as they tried to regain their breathing between jokes. Together Mia and Jilly begin to realize that their new-found friends, Ricky and George, were not met by coincidence, but rather sheer destiny.

Ricky and George are engineering students in the ROTC program and U.S. Air Force candidates. Both men would be the first in their families to graduate college. They met on their first day at SIU Carbondale, and both men consider each other brothers. The men share a common bonded rule, "Don't go anywhere or do anything without the other." They are truly brothers till the end.

Ricky is from Grand Rapids, MN, the hometown of actress of Frances Ethel Gumm who used the stage name of Judy Garland. The small town is known for its timber harvesting and is the base for many paper manufacturers. With over 1,000 lakes in the region, hunting and fishing are commonplace. Ricky is an avid hunter himself and is considered by many as an expert shooter. His shooting is so good that his ROTC training commanding officer wanted to place him in "Sniper Training," but he refused the offer to remain with his friend George instead. During his training, Ricky could hit (Bulls Eye) targets over 2,000 yards away. Handling a sniper rifle came naturally to Ricky as his instructors were amazed at his ability to shoot vast distances without any formal training.

Ricky also possessed the skill of "Tracking" which he used for volunteering at the Fish and Game Commission. His ability to track down wounded game was a rare talent that gave him much satisfaction during weekends as a student. These additional skills could have also been used in his military career, but again, Ricky didn't want to be separated from his friend George.

George is from Holland, MI and loves to fly hot air balloons over the western river valleys of Michigan. The sport was introduced to him by his high school teacher, and since then he has been hooked on ballooning. His favorite ballooning view was to fly over the tulip farms of Holland, Michigan and absorb the almost endless kaleidoscope of colored tulips in full bloom. Hot air ballooning also gave George a special feeling of peace and tranquility when flying high above as he would let his imagination flow free.

As a young boy, George's father taught him ice fishing on Lake Michigan and as he got older, he saw a need for fellow fishermen. Being the very mechanical thinker he was, George designed, built, and sold "Ice Fishing Cabins" to area fishermen. He started building no-frills ice fishing cabins, but soon afterward learned that most fishermen wanted some of the comforts of home in their cabins. George began to add wood burning stoves, beds with mattresses, and low voltage battery lighting. His customers could drag their cabins over a favorite fishing hole on frozen Lake Michigan and fish in a somewhat warm and comfortable setting. This business venture enabled him to save enough money to pay for most of his college costs.

Both men will enter the Air Force as Second Lieutenants after graduation this June. Their Air Force recruiter has submitted their paperwork for them to remain stationed together if they volunteer for a full year tour of duty in Vietnam. Ricky and George want to further extend their education under the GI bill once they complete their Air Force commitments.

The two couples become items and within a few weeks, the four of them are inseparable. Each of them look forward to warmer months when George promises that they will be thrilled to try flying silently high above the landscape. George describes the craving to hear only the wind and feel it flowing over your face as the panoramic view of lakes, rivers, and farmed fields stimulate your mind. Just by hearing those words, the group is sold on hot air ballooning.

The Beatles release "Eleanor Rigby" in the summer of 1966. The months fly by with Ricky and George graduating and leaving for the Air Force officer training in Colorado. The training is intense, and they don't get any time while in training to see the girls for four months. Writing letters between each other becomes the only way to communicate, even though officer boot camp is intense. Classroom training for eight hours, then hard-nose running obstacle courses and marching for another eight hours. With only eight hours left in a day to sleep, eat, study, makes the small task of writing a letter a very hard accomplishment.

What will we do when they are overseas? Where are we going to live? Can we follow them wherever they go? These are some of the questions Mia and Jilly ask themselves. Wondering what they will do when the guys eventually leave for their tour in Vietnam is the question that neither can answer. Both girls are afraid to address Ricky and George with their questions, fearing that it might scare them off. Mia and Jilly are both wanting from their men some sign of commitment. After all, once the guys are stationed overseas, it could be a whole year of waiting. Being the timider of the two, Mia settles on Jilly's suggestion of bringing it up when the four of them are together again.

Upon completing their Air Force training, the guys fly back to Carbondale to see the girls. The reunion is intense and filled with love and promises. At first the guys decide to hold off telling the girls that they have only a week off before they must report to Travis Air Force Base in California. Meeting the girls in their dormitory room isn't the best place to renew their affections, so they decide to check into a motel. Taking two separate rooms adjacent to each other works out to their best interests. In a real way, both couples have so much to make up for and so little time to fulfill their desires.

At breakfast the next morning, being a woman of her word, Jilly brings up the questions her and Mia need answered. George and Ricky were caught a little off guard by Jilly's questions, but both men realize that some sort of future should be made. Telling jokes by George seems to offset the seriousness of the issues and places everyone in a more relaxed mood. It is then suggested by Jilly that her and Mia, upon graduation, will pursue nursing employment near the Travis Base. Ricky thinks it's a great idea, and George seconds the motion. Mia is now all smiles and proposes a toast to their futures as they all raise their cups of coffee in one big clinking sound.

Ricky peeks through an opening in a fence when he hears shouting. The two couples planned a picnic in Carbondale Park that late morning. Early that morning, the girls packed sandwiches, cheese, and crackers along with two bottles of chardonnay wine. The plan was to spend some quiet time together and try to enjoy whatever time they have together before saying their good-byes. The shouting turns into an uproar. Caught laying on a blanket about to open the first bottle of wine, George and Ricky jump up to seek a better view. They see a large group of protesters yelling and holding signs moving in their direction. Ricky is the first to read the signs. He informs the others that they are protesting the Vietnam War. The four are dumbfounded when one of the protesters walks towards them and asks if they want to join the march. Jilly and Mia recognize some of the marchers as fellow students. They had no idea they were planning a demonstration. The thought of the Vietnam War was now swiftly imbedded in each of their minds. Previously omitting the mention of war in any plans will now have to be a force to be reckoned with.

The week passes very quickly, and the girls must say their goodbyes for now. Not standing still for a moment, they have already applied to some nursing facilities. Within just a few days, the first reply comes from The American Red Cross in Fairfield, CA only a few miles away from Travis Air Force Base, which makes the guy's departure a little easier to take. The American Red Cross jobs will pay the girls a third less than any other medical center in the Midwest. But money at this point isn't in their plans and takes a back seat in priority just so long as they all can be together again. Once the guys leave, both couples spend an abundance of time writing letters, trying to keep their close relationship ongoing.

Just before Thanksgiving, Mia suggests that her and Jilly fly out to see Ricky and George in California for Christmas. Willing to dip into her trust funds, Mia is happy to pay Jilly's airfare, and the guys can handle a few days of hotel costs. They can also pay a visit to The American Red Cross and scope out the facilities. The girls arrive on December 22nd in San Francisco and are met by Ricky and George who had no time to change clothing, still wearing their Air Force uniforms. Trying not to capture any attention, Ricky and George parked the car rental and walked through the terminal. The guys were warned about wearing uniforms and confronting anti-war protesters, especially at San Francisco International Airport.

Watching the girls step out of the jetway brings smiles to Ricky and George as they are greeted with kisses and hugs by Mia and Jilly. At the baggage claim area when the girls' two bags are retrieved, the couples start to walk to the parking lot. On their way almost out of the building, they run into Hari Krishna anti-war demonstrators chanting, "Hey, hey, LBJ, how many kids did you kill today." Ricky grabs Mia's hand and George Jilly's as they try to walk around the protesters, but the passageway is narrow. The Hari Krishna group takes note of the two men in uniform and blocks their way while the chanting gets louder. Ricky reaches out to stiff arm an opening to pass through. As he leads the way, he feels a wet sensation on his face. While trying to walk faster, they finally reach the doorway and quickly step outside. When they were clear of the building, Ricky stopped to wipe his face from the dripping saliva. Mia makes the remark, "Why don't they realize you guys are obliged to serve your country, and the war isn't your fault."

Jilly adds, "It's the Politians who are at fault."

Finding an affordable hotel in the San Francisco area landed the couples at the El Camino motel in Daly City, only a short drive to the major points of interest. The girls get a chance to see the facilities of The American Red Cross in Fairfield. They are filled with excitement and can't wait for their assignments. It is a long day filled with visiting Alcatraz, Fishermen's Wharf, and hours of riding cable cars. Everyone decides to go to their rooms early, but the willingness of wanting to share love remains the real reason. That night Mia and Ricky deeply fall in love as their two bodies melt into one. No words need to be spoken between them, only the calling impulse to share their love and desires. For now two strangers in the dark become two passionate lovers, glowing by the soft light of night.

1968

The time has come for the Vietnam War to reach its height. In the early spring, the girls finally finish college, having their nursing degrees in hand accepting their new positions at The American Red Cross. Mia and Jilly feel a little remorse leaving their friends in Carbondale, but don't want to look back, only ahead. With a U-Haul trailer in tow packed to the brim with their worldly possessions, each girl is filled with the excitement of the move. Jilly has already spent some time plotting out their route and makes sure they will have enough non-perishable food and snacks to keep the travel cost down. Catching I-70 west, the girls pass though Missouri, Kansas, Colorado, Utah, Nevada and finally cross the California state line.

Watching the road rushing under the hood of her car as she stares out the windshield, Jilly is almost hypnotized by the waves of amber and the fields of corn. Just as they were passing though the state of Kansas, playing on the radio is the new Beatles song, "A Day in The Life." Jilly wakes Mia from napping so she can also hear the new song. The haunting lyrics of John Lennon singing those words brought their emotions to a crowning of expression as the tears fell from their eyes. There is a sudden newsbreak after the song is played. It is a news report on Vietnam. Operation Junction City, named after Junction City Kansas, is waged by the U.S. Army, and 282 U.S. soldiers are killed. Still teary eyed, Mia looks at Jilly knowing they both are thinking of their guys. Their new song now has an added meaning and purpose as Jilly gazes ahead and notices a road sign reading, "Thank you for visiting Junction City."

Repelling, resisting, fending off are the only words to describe their combined rejection. Each car radio report showboating the war results in the girls not wanting to hear anymore. Jilly turns off the radio and asks Mia to reach under the seat and grab the cassette player. Trying to turn on the tape player, Mia can't get it to work. They figure out the cassette player needs batteries. Getting off the next exit, they find a convenience store and purchase a six pack of Eveready Batteries. Waiting in line to pay, the girls are attracted to the small television hanging from the ceiling behind the cashier tuned to a national news broadcast. The announcement of Martin Luther King being assassinated send chills through the girls' bodies, almost causing Mia to vomit. The store is filled with shocked customers as the news travels around the store.

What's left of the ride to California is accomplished without listening to the radio. Helping to pass the time away, the girls' talk seems to always bring them back to worrying about the effects of the war. Along the way, the girls drum up a heated conversation about how they are going to handle their men away while in the war. Each of them tries to accept the fact that they can't ignore the news and not to believe everything they hear. They wonder what the conditions will be when their boys arrive in Vietnam. There is no open window in their futures and having no control over anything makes them shake inside just by thinking of what lies ahead.

2006 South Vietnam

Towing the line, Chet and Ta reach the last small bridge before entering Tra Vinh province just as local farmers are about to cross at the same time. Chet must pull over to the side shoulder of the road so water buffalo can be herded though. He once again realizes how big a water buffalo is, three times the size of his smart car, and how they are used as plow horses in Vietnam. There are two types of water buffalo: the swamp buffalo, which is grayish with blueish tones, and the river buffalo, which is black in color, and its horns grow down and backward. Each weighing about 1,000 to 1,200 lbs. The river buffalo prefers deeper water and can graze under water for plants. Both are well adapted to a hot and humid climate with temperatures ranging 100 degrees or greater in the summer. Water availability is important in hot climates since the buffalo need wallows, rivers, or splashing water to assist in keeping their body temperatures stable. Some breeds of water buffalo are adapted to saline seaside shores and saline sandy terrain. The Mekong Delta region makes it a perfect place for these water buffalo to work and thrive.

The gurgling sound now surges, almost giving Chet interference in hearing. Driving into the town Tra Vinh, Ta directs Chet to pull alongside a roadside café and stop when Ta then steps out of the car and comes around to the driver's side motioning Chet to follow. Both men walk into the café as Ta gestures to the owner for a menu and tells Chet the food is very good if you like a Micro Asian flare. Perusing the menu quickly, Ta orders two bowls of bun thit nuong and explains that they will be eating an old Vietnamese favorite, grilled pork with oriental vegetables. They decide to drink hot green tea and are given a pot which is placed in the center of their table along with two sipping bowls.

Feeling the heat closing in as they sip their green tea, Ta asks Chet, "Now, tell me why you wanted to be here?" Chet explains that after the passing of his wife, Nancy, he has been hearing a bizarre gurgling sound in his head. He explains that he also heard the very same sound a few days after the typhoon of September 1968 when he was on the My Tho River. Chet then admits that he may be crazy, but he thinks it's a calling for him to respond to something. Seeming surprised Ta studies Chet's eyes as though he can see right into his mind for a response. Their conversation is interrupted by the café owner bringing over their steamy hot bun thit nuong with the aromatic smell making their mouths water. Chet is starving; he has not been eating well ever since his stomach pain flared up, attributing his hunger to feeling better after taking Dr. Diem's potion. They both dig in. Chet enjoys Ta's choice, smiling and softly moaning as he chews and sips his tea.

It begins to rain as the conversation returns to those odd gurgling sounds. Chet covers his ears to helplessly shield the sound. Ta asks, "Where were the sounds the strongest when you were on the river?" Chet replies that he recalls the gurgling calls the closest when he arrived at a small marina or supply depot. Ta's eyes open wide when he hears Chet's answer so much that he just sat up and stared into the distance as though under the deepest of thought. Chet lets the response pass and assumes that Ta knows something that he is holding back from him. Chet asks for the check and then looks at Ta and demands to know what made him act so surprised when he described the location of the gurgling sounds. Ta shakes his head, giving a no answer, but Chet stares him down and gives a look of disgruntlement.

Full of nightmares, Ta confesses to Chet about stealing from the Viet Cong three weeks before a devastating Typhoon hit. At the time he was a young teenage boy hiding out with other orphans, stealing whatever they could to survive. There were three orphans, plus himself being the oldest, who witnessed two young Caucasian women sold to the Viet Cong by well-known kidnapers. Ta describes the kidnapers as sleazy men who made a living in the underground sex slave market. Many of the villages would do their best to try to keep their daughters away, keeping them under constant supervision. The kidnaped girls were usually sold into prostitution, but this special sale, for the first time, included two white Caucasian women. A few days before the sale, Ta watched the Viet Cong build two large bamboo cages. The orphans were thinking at the time that the cages would be used on them if they were caught.

The cages were hung over the river using block and tackle and remained hanging empty for weeks.

It was raining, the sun had just set in the west when the silence of the night was disrupted. The screeching sound of a vehicle coming to an abrupt stop broke the peaceful silence. Very quickly the driver and two helpers jumped out of the van and opened the rear door. From a distance, Ta saw two white women bound and gagged with rope and rags carried to the main Viet Cong hut. Inside the hut, he heard some of the conversation and knew that the kidnapers were not happy when the Viet Cong reneged on the price to pay. An argument broke out with the Viet Cong saying the two women were not military, so the price should be half the amount. The only other thing Ta remembered was that some sort of settlement was reached and the kidnapers, when paid, drove off in a rage.

The girls were imprisoned in the bamboo cages like monkeys. For most of a day they sat in a squatting position with not even enough room to stretch their legs. They remained hanging over the My Tho River and threatened by death if they tried to escape or cry out for help. Whenever someone would pass by in the river, the girls were lowered into the water and forced to use bamboo snorkels for breathing. This made them silent and invisible to any outsider and at the same time, totally helpless.

Through the warm murky water by day and the flowing sounds by night, the river became full of life to the Viet Cong. Ta admits ever since he stole items belonging to the two girls, he started hearing echoing screams at night during full moons. The screaming echoes seemed to always come from the river banks. Ta's strange occurrence went on in his mind for years until he moved to Saigon when he was a young adult after the war. Chet remembers that the "Typhoon Cobra's" super force was made possible by an extreme easterly wind, high tide, and full moon. Ta wonders if there is a connection between the screams he heard and the storm. Chet remembers the morning of September 13th in 1968. Just before Typhoon Cobra arrives, his swift boat was given orders to make one last patrol up river to warn villagers of the approaching typhoon. Ta then asks, "Was your swift boat PCF-33?"

Chet's response was filled with bewilderment as he replies, "How did you know that?"

Ta answers, "I was there, and your boat had a big brown dog aboard who was franticly barking. I was hiding in the river's jungle growth which was something we orphans learned to do very well." As PCF-33 pulled into the old marina, Ta closely watched the Viet Cong respond in a panic mode when they saw the swift boat approach the marina. Ta says he will never forget the chain of events that took place at that moment and firmly believes that the relentless screaming he has been hearing definitely has something to do with that day.

For the two unknown women, their screams echoed cries for help down the river into the jungle, but no one answered the call. The sky above had clouds rushing by as the wind began to gust through the tree line. Ta reaches into his pocket and pulls out a small envelope and cuffs it in the palm of his hand. Facing the ground, he then looks up at Chet who has a surprised expression on his face. Ta's hand slowly extends out to place the envelope in clear view for Chet to see. Chet reaches for the envelope which has some weight to it and seems to contain small metal items jingling together. Chet asks, "What is this?"

Ta responds, "It belongs to you. Ever since we had our discussion at the hotel bar, I knew you were the person to give this to." Chet graciously accepts the envelope and very carefully shakes the contents. Hearing a tinkling sound like small metal bits rattling, he slowly tears open the envelope.

Chapter 6

1968 Fairfield, California

After a brief early morning rain shower, the fallen droplets of rain are quickly absorbed into the thirsty, dry soil. It's now 8 o'clock on a Saturday, and the girls finally arrive at the Shady Brook Motel. The main motel building is neatly painted bright white, two stories high with outdoor entrances to each room. Along the outdoor passageway, there is an orange railing running the length of the building. The office is in a separate small structure also bright white with an orange colored roof giving the impression that it might have at one time been a Howard Johnson Motel. Flashing over the office door is a red 1950's style neon sign spelling "No Vacancies."

For Mia and Jilly, it was wonderful noticing both their guys standing on the second-floor deck taking a smoke break. Mia was driving and leaned on the car horn to surprise Ricky and George who then recognized the girls and both ran to the nearest staircase. When the guys reached the car, the girls jumped out and ran into their arms with flying leaps and immediately kissed with passion. The tears began to flow with happiness as the guys showed some sort of restraint, which the girls immediately picked up on. Ricky suggests that the girls freshen up and they all go to dinner at a place called "Frisco's." Only a mile from the Shady Brook, it was a quiet place serving the finest Italian food. The owner of Frisco's is Rocco Giannini who claimed to be a direct descendent of Amadeo Giannini who founded the Bank of Italy 1904 which became the Bank of America in 1928. Amadeo Giannini is credited as the inventor of many modern banking practices. Most notably Giannini was one of the first bankers to offer banking services to middle-class Americans rather than only the upper class. He also pioneered the holding company structure and established one of the first modern trans-national institutions.

The guys help carry the girls' luggage up to the second floor where they booked two adjacent rooms, 113 and 115. The luggage is dropped on the beds. Mia and Ricky are in room 113, Jilly and George in room 115. The guys step back outside to continue their smoke break while the girls take their quick showers and get out of their sticky road-worn clothes. Before jumping into the shower, Mia knocks on the walk though door between the rooms. Jilly answers the door, already draped in a towel, and looks at Mia and reaffirms that something is wrong with the guys. Both acknowledge that their upbeat men are acting like the weight of the world is on their shoulders.

The crisp night air had the scent of burning wood from Frisco's large stone fireplace. The restaurant is in a white stucco self-standing building that was built around 1900. The two dining rooms are decorated in Italian scenic murals on all four walls. The larger dining room is called "Roma" which shows the ancient ruins of the Roman Colosseum and Pompeii. A smaller dining room called "Amalfi" has painted murals of the rocky cliffs of the Amalfi coast towns including Capri, Sorrento, and Positano.

The couples are greeted and escorted by the owner, Rocco, to a table facing the amber flames radiating just enough heat to remove the chill of the night. George orders a bottle of Chianti wine while the waiter gives them the specials with a broken English-Italian accent. They order a large, cold antipasto for all to share. The girls both are starving and quickly order meat lasagna for Jilly and baked ziti for Mia as entrees. The guys follow with each ordering spaghetti and meatballs. George pours the wine and tells the girls that he and Ricky have something to say. Mia takes a big gulp of her wine, and Jilly eyes fill with tears. Ricky explains with a cracked voice that they both just received their orders for Vietnam and must be on a PSA Airline-Military Air Command (MAC) flight leaving in just ten days. The Air Force personnel office has told them both to get their lives in order and prepare to leave for Vietnam. George then cuts into the conversation by informing the girls that they both will be stationed at "Tan Son Nhut Air Base" just northeast of Saigon.

The girls are shocked as reality starts to set in. They stare at each other with their mouths wide open. Mia then yells out that when they report to their new jobs at the Red Cross, they will request for a change of duty station to Saigon. Jilly also thinks it's a great idea while the guys openly show their discontent by standing up and shaking their heads no, no, and more no. Ricky explains the danger factor by reminding the girls it's a war zone, and U.S Armed Forces are now being attacked on all fronts due to something called The Tet Offensive. George expresses his concern that civilians are no safer than military people. The girls look at each other, both recalling the news reports they heard during the drive to California. Despite the known danger, they secretly won't have it any other way, insisting that they will also go no matter what.

Worried expressions are then turned into stone as the guys' faces are drained of blood, not knowing if the girls will truly follow their wishes. Ricky and George's faces are as white as sheets, and they remained completely dumbfounded with nothing to say. Silence now sets in for all four of them as they stare at each other, waiting for someone to break the ice by speaking. The guys weren't finished with what they had to say before Mia made the comment of following them to Vietnam. George looks at Ricky for some direction, and he obtains a nod of approval. Each guy reaches into their pockets and take out two small velvet boxes. George's box is black, and Ricky's is red. Each guy kneels in front of his girl and opens their small box revealing two gold wedding bands. Mia's band is yellow gold and has the inscription "Love always, Ricky" with Jilly's band in white gold inscribed "Forever my love, George." As though the guys rehearsed their presentation, each simultaneously breaks the ice of silence asking the girls for their hand in marriage. Jilly first hugs Mia and starts to cry while each of them then fall into the arms of George and Ricky saying, "Yes!" Ricky explains that they couldn't afford to buy diamond engagement rings, and both he and George promised the girls formal diamond rings will come.

Leaving Frisco's on the way back to the Shady Brook Motel, Jilly suggests, "Why don't they get married as soon as possible?" Mia seconds the motion by suggesting they drive to Reno, Nevada and get married with Mia, Ricky, and George gasping with joy. That night became a moment in the two couple's lives that will live much longer than anyone of them ever could realize. Jilly says, "If we have each other, there is nothing more we need." George looks at Ricky then submits that in the morning they drive to Reno and get married. The couples raise their empty glasses in making a toast to their future.

Running hard and running blind across Interstate 80, they pay no attention to the beautiful vistas of rock formations lined with sequoia pine. The majestic beauty of the rough cut and jagged mountains along the ride have no special interest to anyone in the group. George for some reason is thinking there is a time limit, wanting to arrive before the girls change their minds. With only a three-hour ride along the regal Sierra Nevada mountains, the two couples streak through Donner's Pass as though it didn't even exist.

Once in Reno, they pull off interstate 80 when a billboard advertising The Starlight Cottages, "a cozy place." catches their attention. They check in and share a double unit with two bedrooms facing the highest mountain within sight. The sun is shining brightly, and the rays are bouncing off the ground while giving a crimped illusion to the dry landscape.

Jilly finds a telephone book in the cottage and looks up wedding chapels while Mia comes running in with her transistor radio playing The Beatles "In My Life." Mia and Jilly turn to each other with a glowing expression of love while realizing that they are now living in the words of the song. They stop what they were doing and join in, singing along with the meaningful lyrics as they get teary eyed. Ricky and George absorb the moment as they witness the closeness of friendship between the two girls.

> There are places I'll remember
> All my life, though some have changed
> Some forever, not for better
> Some have gone and some remain
> All these places have their moments
> With lovers and friends, I still can recall
> Some are dead and some are living
> In my life, I've loved them all
> But of all these friends and lovers
> There is no one compares with you
> And these memories lose their meaning
> When I think of love as something new

Though I know I'll never lose affection
For people and things that went before
I know I'll often stop and think about them
In my life, I love you more
Though I know I'll never lose affection
For people and things that went before
I know I'll often stop and think about them
In my life, I love you more
In my life, I love you more

A scream is sounded across the cottage when the girls notice an ad for a wedding chapel located on the banks of Lake Tahoe. Sequoia Pines Chapel offers romantic views, quick ceremonies, and honeymoon cottages with no reservations needed. All in agreement, the next morning after breakfast, the four check out of the Starlight. Driving south for about forty-five miles, easily finding the chapel nestled amongst seventy-five-foot-tall pine trees. Ricky and George sitting in the front seat, step out of the car first having the girls wait until they are called. Jilly jumps in the front seat and restarts her car and immediately turns on the radio. Mia then asks Jilly if she is totally committed to what they are about to do. Jilly remarks that she has never been happier in her life as Mia reaches out for her hand and replies, "So am I."

After about twenty minutes, the guys return with great big smiles on their faces and usher the girls into the small chapel painted periwinkle blue with white lace trim. Standing in front of the altar are the owners of the chapel, Fred and Margaret Owens, who have been operating the chapel for over twenty years. The road signage for Sequoia Pines Chapel also has an add on smaller sign stating that appointments are taken for "Fortune Telling by Mother Margaret."

The backdrop of the altar is filled with the locally grown flowers Scarlet Pimpernel, Heartleaf Arnica, Parish Goldeneye, and Sugar Brush Mariposa. The flowery arrangements offer the couples a feeling of being in The Garden of Eden, and the fragrances send their senses into a sacred spiritual place. The church wedding song, "Bridal Chorus," is provided by a tape player.

The wedding service is simple and speedy while the couples take their vows per traditional readings and pledge, "To have and to hold, from this day forward, for better, for worse, for richer, for poorer, in sickness and in health until death do us part." Fred Owens pronounces them husbands and wives and closes with, "You may kiss the brides." George and Ricky embrace their wives and hold a long kiss which seemed like it was endless. Very softly in the background the couples hear the song "Somewhere Over the Rainbow" nicely finalizing the end of their ceremony. As the two couples walk toward the end of the aisle, they are greeted by Margaret Owens. She speaks out to say congratulations, but also makes the comment, "My vibes tell me that you are all special people who radiate something unusual that I can't right now place my finger on."

That night the newlywed couples shared all the love they had for each other. For Mia and Jilly, it was a night they lived for only in their dreams, but now it was real. The rhythm of love making softly resounded throughout the tiny cottage. Candlelight glowed in the dark casting romantic shadows against the walls. For the moment, the birth of love seized its place over the fears which lie ahead.

Over the next few days while honeymooning at the cottages, the couples would catch a glimpse of Margaret Owens looking at them with a strange, puzzled expression. Mia and Jilly were starting to freak out about Margaret constantly gawking at them, giving them the impression that she could see into their future. But it was pushed aside by Ricky and George saying that she was just a crazy person. Between the two impressions, Mia and Jilly accept the guys' view of Margaret. More importantly it is time for the couples to look ahead and plan the next chapter in their lives.

The girls placed phone calls to assure themselves an apartment in Fairfield thanks to the help of Ricky and George's fellow Air Force buddies. A rented U-Haul trailer filled with their belongings is still parked at the Shady Brook Motel. Having the apartment will please the Shady Brook management since it can now be moved and unloaded when they return. Their time together was swiftly passing, approaching the time the guys had to return to base. Finally it came time to check out of Sequoia Pines and load up the car. Passing by the office for the last time on their way out, Margaret Owens is standing by the door watching them leave with a haunting look on her face. Jilly comments, "She's giving me the creeps," and Mia says, "Me too." Ricky quickly accelerates, honks the horn, and Margaret waves goodbye. With only clouds of dust blocking out the images of the cottages in the rearview mirror, their stay is now just a memory.

Later that same night, screams in the still of the night are reverberating from the main cottage at Sequoia Pines. Margaret is awakened in a cold sweat from a deep sleep with a nightmarish dream. In the dream, she sees rushing tides, crashing waves, and flooding water. Margaret also hears gusting winds and gurgling echoes in her nightmare, recalling the frightful site of the "Angel of Death" silhouette holding the hands of two women. She realizes that her bad vibes have something to do with the two girls who checked out earlier in the day.

Passing back over Donner's Pass, Ricky decides to make a pit stop as he follows a sign in the distance for a Union 76 gas station. Off to the side, Jilly and Mia have a private conversation concerning keeping their maiden names. They both agree by keeping their own family names, their career goals will not be disturbed. When they explain their decision, at first Ricky and George are complexed about the concept of keeping their maiden names. The girls clarify that by doing so opportunities for advancement will be greater. Mia relays that by the time the guys are finished with their Air Force commitment, she and Jilly will have taken full advantage of their own career aspirations, and then it would finally be a good time to use their new married names. Reluctantly the guys agree, but want to leave the matter on the table for a future discussion.

Jilly calls her mom to let her know the good news while Mia shares the receiver and joins in on the conversation. Due to the time difference, Jilly's father, Dave, is working and not home. Edith is totally surprised by the news of them getting married so soon after meeting the guys. Jilly gives her mom the bad news about George and Ricky receiving their orders for Vietnam. Edith becomes silent when Jilly gives her the news that she and Mia will soon follow the guys to Vietnam. Crying out loud is the only release Edith has, and her mild composure is destroyed. Jilly and Mia joined in crying with Edith. Several minutes later when the three reach a point of being able to speak, Edith comments that her and Dave always looked forward to a church wedding where Dave could walk Jilly down the aisle. Edith reminds Jilly that she and her father yearned for a formal wedding reception for their oldest daughter. She realizes this yearning is now nothing more than a lost dream. Ali hears her mother crying and asks what is wrong. After Edith attempts to compose herself and tries not to send the wrong message in her answer. She slowly searches to find the delicate words to explain that Jilly and Mia have married. Edith describes to Ali that both are extremely in love and have married in Reno, followed by a long pause, and finally mentioning they will follow their husbands to Vietnam. Loving sister Ali immediately grabs the phone from her mom's ear, screaming with joy for Jilly and Mia to hear. After Edith realizes her harsh tone conveyed to Jilly and Mia, she realizes she was wrong. Displaying remorse she takes the phone back. Edith succumbs to the fact that she can't change a thing and wishes them only happiness. Once again Edith begins to cry uncontrollably. Jilly and Mia promise Edith and Ali that they will be cautious and careful while abroad and remind her that they will not be in harm's way. Mia jumps into the conversation with Edith, bringing up the fact that The American Red Cross will keep them safe. Edith closes her discussion stating that she hopes that God will look over them. The girls promise to write often and keep in touch. In unison their final words to Edith are, "We love you, Mom."

Ali, now realizing how emotionally upset Edith is about the girl's safety, tries to comfort her mom with loving words and the thought of Jilly and Mia being the two happiest people she knows. Expressing her own feelings, Ali admits to Edith that she misses her sisters and feels that their love for each other will help keep them safe. Through all the tears, Ali stares into her mom's eyes and says, "You and Dad can have that big fancy wedding moment when I get married." Ali finds that it is a good time to ask for her mother's hand in pray. They both hold on to each other and bow their heads, asking the lord to watch over the two couples and all those who are in harm's way.

Boxes still waiting to be unpacked in their apartment, the sorrow of saying goodbye remains. The night before the guys are leaving, each couple stays tightly bound within their bedrooms. At times the tones of love making are substituted with the sounds of grieving. Both couples don't want the night to end, consequently allowing the tides of passion to take over. As the moments together slowly slip by, the couples have no idea just how precious this final night is.

Bright and early the next morning as Ricky and George dress in their formal Air Force uniforms, the girls slip into casual clothes. Jilly and Mia seem to be comatose in spirit. The guys sense the tension and want to relieve the pressure, wishing time would move on more quickly. The guys want to leave as soon as possible considering their prolonged presence with the girls an obstacle. The last thing the men want is to see their loving wives in emotional pain.

During World War II, the United States military transport could not meet all the logistical needs to win a war. Thus the Civil Reserve Air Fleet (CRAF) was developed to use commercial airline capacity to provide maximum airlift support in wartime situations. As a benefit, commercial airlines that committed planes to CRAF could receive peacetime government contracts in an amount proportional to the airline's potential wartime mobilization value. This is the basis for most routine military charter flights. The government receives an extremely economical source of emergency capacity as well as reasonable costs for peacetime military transportation. The major commercial airlines used for moving freight were Flying Tiger Airlines, Overseas National, and World Airways. The major commercial players for moving passengers were Pam Am World Airways, Northwest Orient Airlines, and Pacific Southwest Airlines (PSA). During the mid to late 1960's to the early 1970's, the major hub for most military charters for the Vietnam war was Travis Air Force Base.

George assumes the position of designated driver to Travis AFB with Ricky in the passenger front seat and the girls in the rear seat. The ride is only fifteen minutes away. The large Boeing 707 is off to the side along "Terminal A" with other PSA Airline aircrafts, their blue and red logos shining in the sunlight. George parks the car just behind the side gate entrance to the terminal and pops the trunk. The girls continue to show their sorrow, and Ricky asks them both if they are okay. George stops what he is doing, turns to the girls, and reminds them that this is the easy part, saying goodbye. Knowing what it will be like when they are gone many months on end, Jilly and Mia shrug their shoulders while agreeing with George's words of wisdom. Each couple embrace while kissing and saying the words "I love you," which are repeated over and over. The men grab their bags and walk through the guarded gate. Both girls understand that no civilians are allowed past that point. Ricky and George don't turn back until they climb the rolling steps to the entrance of the plane, finally looking back, blowing kisses, and saluting goodbye. Sniffling, Jilly and Mia shiver in the cool breeze blowing from the west, continuing to wave their own goodbyes.

The PSA flight plan calls for stopping in Honolulu, Wake Island, and Clark Air Force Base in the Philippines where Ricky and George will finally transfer to a small C1A which will take them to Saigon. The plane crew waits for other passengers and when all are aboard, quickly taxies to the runway and out of sight. Flying through several time zones and the International Dateline, Ricky and George will arrive at Clark Air Force Base the very same day and time they left Travis. Reliving February 2nd twice does nothing but revive their joyous moments of the past ten days with their wives.

From Mia and Jilly's view, being strong, independent women will help them accept the absence of their husbands. In what seems to have happened in the blink of an eye, their futures undefined, at least they have each other.

There is nothing but silence on the car ride back to the Shady Brook Motel where they will check out for the last time and move into their apartment. The move goes easier than expected when five Air Force buddies of Ricky and George show up to help the girls move. Mia and Jilly are reassured by the five that all will be okay since the guys' duties will not involve direct confrontation with the enemy. One of the five buddies named Bronson made the comment, "It's not like Ricky and George are grunts fighting in rice paddies." The reference doesn't console the girls especially since current TV news reports showing the North Vietnamese Army and Viet Cong attacking both military and civilian targets. Mia tells the group of buddies, "Stop talking about Vietnam! It's giving me chills just hearing the slightest mention of that stupid war."

The next Monday, Mia and Jilly report to their new jobs at The American Red Cross, filling out paperwork and attending orientation meetings. While in the personnel office, Jilly mentions to the department head that both she and Mia would like to transfer to Saigon so they can be closer to their husbands. The department manager responds to the request with a sorrowed expression on her face and tells the girls it may take a month or two for processing. She further explains why it will take so long. The Red Cross must be very careful before they transfer people to Vietnam. Since the "Tet Offensive" started a few weeks ago, the orders from Washington have been changing almost daily.

The girls begin working together as registered nurses on the night shift. It's a hard day's night working long hours, six days a week. The schedule is grueling, but the long hard work keeps their minds off thinking about all the wicked war news. They finally realize for the first time how much they love nursing. They feel very fortunate that they chose nursing as their profession. The importance of caring for the sick and hurt is extremely important to both Mia and Jilly. They feel a sense of accomplishment watching their patients heal. The girls start to see the wounded from Vietnam pass through their infirmary. It's hard for them to contain their emotions while treating these patients, especially soldiers with lost limbs or burns. At certain times holding back their tears is completely impossible while also thinking of Ricky and George's safety.

It has now been a stretch of long, lonely days since the guys departed for Vietnam. Mia decides to check their mailbox located at the bottom of the hallway staircase and is jolted with surprise after she pulls out some junk mail. In the middle of the junk mail pile, she finds two letters marked "FREE" in place of postage stamps. During the Vietnam War, all military personnel could send an unlimited amount of first class letters back home for free. The word "Free" had to be written in the upper right-hand corner of the envelope in place of a postage stamp. This program applied to all branches of the military serving in country or serving in the Gulf of Tonkin. All Army and Air Force personnel used an Army Post Office Box (APO) return address in San Francisco, CA. The Navy and Marines used a Fleet Post Office Box (FPO) also in San Francisco.

One letter is addressed to Mia from Ricky, and the other is addressed to Jilly from George. Mia's screeching yell of happiness from the bottom of the steps is so loud that all the other tenants in the building open their doors to see what made that sound. She apologized to her neighbors while running, taking two steps at a time back to the second floor. Jilly hears all the commotion and opens the apartment door, meeting Mia at the second-floor landing. Jilly is already jumping for joy while not knowing what is happening. With an immense smile on her face Mia hands Jilly the letter from George. She places it over her heart and bows her head as though she was thanking God.

Both the letters provide the girls with a much needed connection of devotion with their husbands. The loving sensation felt by reading their letters places them in a state of ecstasy. Each word of the two letters is absorbed into their subliminal minds as though it was handcrafted and chiseled by Michelangelo himself. But what the girls seem to miss are the words of Ricky and George explaining their wish for the girls not to come to Saigon. The guys give a clear detailed report of the dangers, and together they plead to Mia and Jilly to stay stateside. The guys are sure that their tour of duty will pass quickly, and when finished they can once again reunite back in Travis. The special requests fall on deaf ears and instead gives both the girls a boost to be closer to their men. They can't wait to be approved for duty in Saigon.

The next day, Mia and Jilly go shopping for items the girls sense are needed by Ricky and George through their letters. Stopping at a local Rexall Drug store, they pick up toiletries such as shaving cream, razors, deodorant, tooth paste, and soap. Finding a well-made cardboard box to firmly hold the toiletries and filling it out with canned food items make a nice first care package for Ricky and George. They also send newspapers and magazines. At the last minute, Mia threw in a couple salamis thinking that a dried salami would survive the trip inside the box even though it would take about two weeks before they received it. About three weeks later, they received a letter from their husbands thanking them for the care packages, but reveal that the contents of the packages were coated with an oily stinky substance that was finally determined to be molten salamis. The girls are reminded by their husbands not to send any type of perishable item, especially since packages can sit at airfields in squelching heat with temperatures reaching well over 100 degrees.

By April 1968, the war news is not getting any better. The media begins to verify the escalation of the war by showcasing actual video footage of the jungle fighting. Each negative news report is ignored by the girls as they quickly change the subject. The girls continue to push for their transfers by checking in with the personnel department almost daily. When the actual paperwork finally arrives, the girls are informed they must prepare to leave in two weeks on May 10th. The news is accepted by the girls with the highest level of anticipation, and they begin to arrange and pack for their new adventure together. They are told that they will be traveling with only one Navy type sea bag each. The bag is only able to hold some limited civilian clothing, shoes, and a few Red Cross nursing uniforms. A Navy sea bag is made of Army green heavy-duty canvas shaped like cylinder measuring three feet high and two feet wide. The bag has one large strap sewed into the bag at one end and a metal clip at the other end. When the sea bag is fully packed, the clip locks into a ring at the top of the cylinder locking it closed. The long strap makes carrying the bag easier when placed over a person's shoulder.

The girls decide not to worry Ricky or George by writing to advise them of the news that their transfers have been approved. Holding firm with their secret, Mia and Jilly firmly believe not telling their husbands is the best way to handle the matter. They agree that after they arrive in Saigon will be a much better time to inform the boys of their arrival in Vietnam.

Jilly schedules a call home to Edith and Ali during a certain time of day, purposely avoiding her dad being home thus evading his strong verbal disapproval. The conversation goes well, but Edith doesn't convey her actual feelings about their departure. The girls sense Edith's absent emotions and odd behavior on the phone but chalk it up to her "just being a worried mom." Ali closes the conversation by telling them that she will pray for their safety and looks forward to them all being together again in Peshtigo playing Beatles records. Their strong commitment to ignoring the fact that the war wasn't a place for them continues to get worse day by day.

Jilly finds a nearby twenty-four-seven storage unit that is big enough to hold both girls' household items, clothing, and Jilly's 1962 Ford Falcon. They call the same gang of Air Force buddies to help them move their possessions, but this time they have everyone swear to secrecy to not mention a word to Ricky or George. They all agreed with the girls' request under the misbelief that George and Ricky are totally onboard with them going to Saigon. Continuing their lie that all this would be just an early arrival is accepted by all group.

The American Red Cross office in Fairfield, California hands over special written orders to Mia and Jilly to make sure their inoculations are current. Mia must be given seven vaccines at once and Jilly only three. The girls are each issued two military type notched dog tags with stainless steel linked chains accompanied by an odd shaped metal object. Each dog tag is inscribed with their last name, first name, American Red Cross (ARC) service number, blood type, and religion. They are supplied with instructions to wear one dog tag with the supplied chain around their neck and the other is to be carried on their person always. The directions seem a little odd to the girls, so they ask the personnel manager why? When they hear the response, "In the field of battle, they may be asked to place the second dog tag into one of their boots, which will help identify a detached leg." Mia leans toward Jilly as though she is about to faint, but Jilly grabs her shoulder to reaffirm their motive for going. Jilly asks what is this used for, pointing to the odd shaped metal object. It is explained that it is a P-38 which is used to open "k rations" cans (individual daily combat food rations) taking 38 twists to reach a full rotation of the can. It was originally designed to be carried in a soldier's pocket which is where the "P" came from. During WWII the design was changed to be worn with "Dog Tags" on a chain around the neck.

Noticing the notch on the personnel manager's dog tag, Mia holds hers up asking why her tags don't have one. It is explained that the notch is something needed by medical staff when using the Addressograph labeling machine model 70 for transferring medical records, but the newer issued tags don't have the notch any longer. The personnel manager also reminds them not to take any jewelry with them. Jilly asks if a wedding band is okay, and the girls express a sigh of relief when they are given a yes signal.

On May 10th, the forty first day of spring, Mia wakes up in the morning not feeling well. Jilly takes her temperature which reveals a reading of 103 and suggests that Mia take a double dose of aspirin. Their diagnosis points to Mia's reaction to the large amount of vaccines given just the day before. The last thing they want now is something stupid, like a fever, stopping their trip. Jilly reminds Mia to take the bottle of aspirin along in her purse while traveling.

Jilly calls for a taxi. The brief ride to Travis Air Force Base for their departing flight is on the exact same PSA charter plane and terminal the guys left from. The flight plan is also the same, and the girls find out that most military personnel traveling to Vietnam by air departing from the west coast fly that route. Boarding the Boeing 707 is quick without any noticeable conversations between the mostly military passengers. All branches of the armed forces are aboard facing forward, no one looking to the rear of the plane or even checking their surroundings. Most of the military passengers are in Army uniforms followed by the Marines, Navy, Air Force, and two Coast Guard. Mia then points out to Jilly, standing behind them toward the rear of the plane, are three women wearing American Red Cross uniforms. Jilly takes a quick look and responds by saying she doesn't believe they are nurses. The head flight attendant who had a gold stripe in her hat quickly did a seat count to make sure all seats were filled. She then walked toward the door and forcefully slammed it shut making a sound so loud, it startled Mia.

The look of anguish on the soldiers faces seems to be part of the uniform of the day. The girls still don't comprehend any of the soldier's expressions for the dangers that lie ahead. Never once did it ever occur to Mia or Jilly that some of the passengers sitting on that plane may have not wanted to go to war. The thought of any one of those passengers never coming home was an unseen sign of their emotions. It's as though they were living in a different world.

Mia asks Jilly if she can get the flight attendant's attention. It takes some time, but Jilly finally gets the attendant's attention, and Mia requests a cold wash cloth and some ice. Her fever is spiking while her complexion has lost all its pinkish tone leaving Mia to look white as a ghost. Once the ice and wash cloth arrive, Mia places it on her forehead and releases a loud sigh of relief startling the three Navy sailors sitting in the next row, causing them to stare at Mia. Jilly sinks into her seat and covers her face as though she doesn't want to attract the slightest bit of attention.

Weariness caused by sitting for hours on end takes its toll, and Mia and Jilly finally fall fast asleep. Soon they are jolted awake by the pilot's announcement of a final approach to Clark Air Force Base. Just the thought of being able to stretch their legs after a twenty-four-hour flight gives them a sense of relief. After deplaning and obtaining their sea bags, officials direct them to a bus to take them to their barracks. The temperature is well over 98 degrees, but the Philippine humidity makes it feel a lot worst. The wooden barracks were left over from World War II and were once occupied by both U.S. Marines and Japanese prisoners of war. There was no air conditioning, not even a fan. Their bedding was comprised of a metal rack with what appeared to be a two-inch thick mattress filled with straw. The showers were commune-type lacking privacy, which made the girls feel extremely uncomfortable. The base was surrounded by twelve-foot-high metal fencing with curls of barbed wire layered on top. If the girls didn't know they were in a United States Air Base, they would have thought it was a concentration camp. The plan was to eat a meal and try and get a good night sleep despite the unbearable heat and mosquitos. Mia remarked to Jilly, "I wonder what the boys' living conditions are like in Vietnam."

Jilly quickly replies, "A hell of a lot worse." The girls' final flight was to leave within twenty-four to forty-eight hours shorty before sunrise. They are told that the duty watch person will wake them up on their departure date at 3 am. With the flight leaving at 4:30am, this gives them plenty of time to get acquainted with some of the other women traveling to Saigon.

For Mia and Jilly, this wasn't a time to mingle with the larger group of women. Their isolation was interrupted when one of the other women introduced herself as Sharon Onstadt. She explained that all twelve of the women travelling with Mia and Jilly are known as "Donut Dollies," and they are traveling to Saigon under Red Cross authority. Jilly and Mia weren't familiar with the term and asked, "What is a Donut Dollie?" Sharon describes them as volunteers whose mission is to help the troops forget about the war. Equipped with nothing but cookies, donuts, and the occasional home-style entertainment program. Sharon describes a job that almost seems impossible to accomplish in guerilla warfare. Most of the girls in the group are there because they have a passion for helping people. In Sharon's case, she is a talented singer who wants to entertain the troops. She has held practice sessions with some of the other girls back in the states to prepare for her tour. Sharon offers to try and persuade the other three girls, who together call themselves "The Rockin Dollies," to sing. Mia suggests something from the Beatles. Sharon replies, "Yes, we can. How about their song "I Want to Hold Your Hand?" Jilly and Mia look at each other with a surprised look of acceptance.

It turns out that Mia has much in common with Sharon, who was born in Tucson, AZ but as a child moved to Hannibal, MO just on the other side of the Mississippi River. Sharon has an aunt who lives in Quincy and spent many weekends and an occasional summer there. Grammy's house was only a few blocks from Sharon's aunt's house, and both are sure they must have known each other. After showering and making their beds, the group decides to play charades to pass the time. Gathered in one big circle, sitting and hanging over bunk beds, the girls begin with funny words to be guessed. Within a short time, everyone is laughing uncontrollably as the game transcends from sexy words, to sexier words, and finally to extremely spicy words. The laughing gets so loud it sounds like screaming. Soon a security guard runs into the barracks wondering what is going on. The group immediately holds back their laughter by clamping their hands over their mouths, but it becomes too hard to hold back when someone shouts out the word castration. Laughter is now echoing off the high ceilings while the security guard shakes his head in disbelief which only brings the laughing to its highest crest. Totally worn out, the girls break up the game, and everyone turns in for the night except for Mia, Jilly, and Sharon.

So not to wake up the others, the three begin a whispered conversation which covers their individual lives. Mia mentions that her and Jilly have requested nursing duty in Saigon so they can be closer to their husbands. All the other women are not married, and Sharon is a little shocked when she hears that they are. Jilly lets the cat out of the bag about their husbands not being aware that they are coming, and that George and Ricky begged them to stay stateside. Sharon is in complete shock over what she just heard and sits there thinking in silence. Mia and Jilly wonder why Sharon's demeanor changed so quickly. Sharon turns her head, looking to see if any of the other girls may have been listening, but all the other donut dollies are already sleeping.

Sharon's reason for being upset was that she prided herself on never holding back anything from a husband. Pushing aside a husband's special request is foolish and in Sharon's mind, totally inconceivable. Sharon is perplexed and interprets Mia and Jilly's nonchalant attitude as though they were taking a trip to Disneyland instead of war torn Vietnam. Sharon can't understand why these girls are going without letting their husbands know. "Don't they understand the dangers?" Sharon considers waking up the others so they as a group can help talk some sense into Mia and Jilly. Instead Sharon feels it may be too late to change their minds and continues to stand in silence. Unknown to Sharon is that Mia and Jilly are living in a dream world where they surprise their husbands, finish their tours together, and return home to live happily ever after.

Finally breaking her silence, Sharon begins to tell a story of her being romantically involved with a guy named Jimmy Baxter during her high school days. They dated on a steady basis for a few years, and Jimmy wanted to get married right after high school graduation. Sharon felt that her life to that point had been extremely sheltered. She had a strong desire to travel and experience what life had to offer before she made the commitment of marriage. She also yearned for the opportunity to pursue her singing talents. Sharon relayed that she wanted to see if her singing was good enough to blossom into a professional career and felt that marriage at that time would just get in the way. Sharon admitted she loved Jimmy very much, but needed to experience a life outside of her small town before heading back home and settling down.

Tired of laughing and talking, the three girls finally fall asleep and within a few short hours, the bugle call of reveille sounded across the barracks. All the girls were very slow getting out of their racks, especially Mia, Jilly and Sharon. Going to sleep at 3 am and reveille sounding at 6 am had given them only a few hours of rest. They felt totally exhausted even before the day began. After breakfast the group was told that the donut dollies would be departing for Da Nang instead of Saigon. The change of plans is announced without any explanation. The donut dollies are told that there are beautiful beaches within a short distance of where they will be stationed. They are disappointed hearing the news that they are not going to Saigon, but happy when they learn that they will be close to one of the most famous beaches in Vietnam called China

Beach. Their flight leaves in three hours, which does not give them much time to do anything other than pack their bags and head for their plane.

While packing Sharon convinces her three singing counterparts to sing one last song in acapella for Mia and Jilly. The girls line up four across, clear their throats, and begin to sing "I Want to Hold Your Hand" with Sharon as the lead singer. Instead of hearing the words and harmony of Paul McCartney and John Lennon singing the lyrics, Mia and Jilly hear Sharon's beautiful, melodious voice. The Rockin Dollies version was somewhat different than the Beatles, but the girls loved the slower tempo and combined harmony. Mia and Jilly now agree that Sharon made the right decision to pursue her singing career.

The donut dollies are all packed and set to go when Jilly asked them to pose for a picture. Dressed in Red Cross uniforms, the eleven girls walk outside and over to an empty Huey helicopter sitting off to the side. As many of the Dollies as possible pile into the Huey, and those who can't fit stand alongside and strike a pose for the camera. After the picture is taken, Sharon tosses her instamatic camera to Jilly to take another picture so that Sharon can share it with the group. Their goodbyes begin and end with lots of hugs with some girls having tears in their eyes. During the night, Sharon couldn't sleep just thinking about Mia and Jilly's effort to disguise their arrival in Vietnam with their husbands. At this point, anger starts to run through Sharon's mind, and she tries hard to hold back her deepening feelings of something really bad happening to two people who don't have a clue of the danger that lies ahead.

The next morning Sharon walks over to Mia and Jilly as they prepare to leave and gives them a double hug while saying to them, "Please, please! Promise me that you two will call your husbands today to let them know you are coming." Mia and Jilly nod their heads yes. Sharon turns around and begins to walk away with the dreadful feeling that the girls will not comply with their promise.

Mia and Jilly have the intention to place the call to Tan Son Nhut Air Base to complete their promise, but are suddenly called to report to the infirmary. When they arrive, the girls are informed that a wounded pilot, who was on his way back to the states, has taken a turn for the worse. Mia and Jilly's assistance is needed to try and save the pilot's life. Clark Air Force base is short on nursing staff, and the girls are quickly readied to assist in the operating room. After three hours of intense surgery and three pints of blood, the pilot's vital signs begin to hold. The staff surgeon declares the operation a success and has the pilot sent to the recovery room. The surgeon thanks

* Dog Tags & Wedding Bands

Mia and Jilly for helping him save the pilot's life. The girls are gracious and note that they were both trained for exactly this type of surgery. The surgeon asks Mia and Jilly, "Where are you both headed?"

Jilly responds, "The American Red Cross in Saigon to be near our husbands."

The surgeon then says, "I guess then you both wouldn't consider being stationed here in Clark." Mia answers, "No, sir, we have jumped through many hurdles just to be near our husbands."

The surgeon says, "I didn't think so, but it didn't hurt to ask. If you change your minds, I'm Colonel Lewis, and I would be proud to have you both here serving with me and my staff."

Mia and Jilly are filled with a sense of accomplishment. Their hearts are thumping as they feel their souls on fire with satisfaction. Saving a life is something Mia and Jilly consider the holy grail of being a nurse and the final fulfillment of their vows. Mia tells Jilly, "I was told that the pilot's name is James Rizzo who is married with two young children."

Jilly replies, "Doesn't this moment make you feel warm and fuzzy inside?"

Mia says, "Yes, Jilly, it does, and I'm so happy we did it together."

Because of their assisting Colonel Lewis, time runs out, and the call station is now closed which will not give the girls the time to call their husbands. They are worn out and exhausted and decide to go to sleep early for their early morning flight to Saigon.

The next morning, boarding the C-1A aircraft in the dark was quite an experience for the girls. Stepping into the plane, the girls were instructed to put on parachutes. Hearing the announcement, Mia and Jilly look at each other with puzzlement. A Master Sergeant holds up a parachute and explains how to wear and secure the strapping belts and to make sure it faces the correct way. The Master Sergeant then points out the dangling ring which is pulled down to allow the parachute to open. An attached yellow watertight light is then introduced to the girls, which has a switch to activate the blinking light. Mia and Jilly are told that most of the flight time will be over water, and their parachutes are specially equipped to also serve as life jackets. He then tells the girls that this is all for safety, and they will probably not have to bail out, but if they did, they will be prepared.

Mia and Jilly are beginning to feel frightened realizing this is not a drill, and the dangers are for real. They have come a long way so far without feeling the actual consequences of being in a war zone. Their brushing aside the dangers ahead are now beginning to take root in their minds as fear now fills those voids.

The C-1A seating arrangement was also unique as everyone faces the rear of the plane. While moving into her seat, Mia begins to nervously shake. She tells Jilly that in the past, if forced to face to the rear on trains and buses, she always became violently ill. Thinking it will help, Jilly grabs Mia's hand, and they moved to the last two seats in the rear of the plane. Mia breaks out into a cold sweat as she begins to think about the long flight sitting backwards. Jilly orders her to only look straight ahead and not turn around while in flight. Jilly covered the porthole window with a magazine and hoped that her friend will make it to Saigon without any further signs of illness. Mia closed her eyes while Jilly watched. Mia quickly falls asleep, and Jilly breathes a sigh of relief. Jilly knew that if the plane crew realized that Mia was sick, they would have had her removed, forcing them to be separated.

Once in the air, the vibration of the plane places her into a deep sleep. Luckily the weather was clear so there was no turbulence to further upset Mia. The plane touched ground in a little over two and a half hours. During the flight, time passed very slowly for Jilly as she prayed for Mia to recover prior to landing in Saigon.

Arriving at the American Red Cross facilities in Saigon placed Jilly in a better state of mind. Mia's fever had broken, and she was feeling a bit better, showing signs of her old self. After receiving their work schedule, the girls decide that they will write Ricky and George later that night. Formal paperwork and interviews must be completed before they will have time to sit down and carefully word their letters to their husbands. Putting off notifying their husbands doesn't seem to faze the girls in the least. The girls continue to believe that waiting until the last minute to inform their husbands of their arrival will result in them accepting the fact that they are working in Vietnam and will be able to see them more often. While all of this is transpiring, unbeknownst to Mia and Jilly, letters from the guys to Mia and Jilly are mistakenly stamped and returned to them as "addressee moved left no forwarding address" even though the girls filled out a change of address forms with the US Post Office in Fairfield.

The Red Cross branch manager in charge of nurses, Betty Santos, gives the girls a tour of the facilities and explains that they would be sourced out to any medical unit within a fifty-mile radius that needed their help. The dangers were clearly explained to the girls, and Betty gives them some personal advice. "Always be aware of your surroundings and be suspicious towards everyone. Remember we are in a war zone where the enemy doesn't wear a uniform." Betty also mentions that it is mandatory to sign out when leaving the building, always noting their exact expected return time. Lastly Betty covers the rules regarding the midnight curfew in effect due to the high alert conditions noting there will be no exceptions to the rule. The girls are asked to pose for a photo scrapbook that Betty is compiling to chronical her three years in the Saigon nursing unit. A portrait shot of Mia then another for Jilly with the final picture of both girls standing arm in arm together. Betty remarks, "Beautiful ladies!"

Once unpacked, showered, and settled in, the girls decide to go out and celebrate while discussing their options for the least possible negative reaction from the guys. They don't want to be perceived as liars and clearly want to express what they did was for love. The girls, dressed in civilian clothes, decide to walk down to Tu Do Street just a few blocks from the Red Cross building. Jilly and Mia are wearing dog tags around their necks, and Mia decides to also wear her American Red Cross pin while Jilly doesn't bother wearing hers. Walking down the hallway towards the front entrance, Mia suddenly remembers that they failed to log out. Jilly remarks, "Come on, it'll be only an hour or so; they won't even miss us." As they arrive in the dense commercial area, the noise level becomes almost unbearable with loud 1960's music blasting from numerous street bars. The street is filled with all types of soldiers, sailors, and airmen from many different countries having a good time without any signs of war. They are completely surprised by the complete chaos of the traffic flow in Saigon. Red traffic signals are disregarded by motorist in all directions. At one point while attempting to cross Tu Do Street, Mia's left foot is almost run over by a speeding scooter. Despite all the bedlam, the girls feel that they are in a safe place and begin to be absorbed by their surroundings. To their surprise, they hear in the distance the playing of another favorite Beatles song "A Day in the Life" coming from a roof top location with a blinking blue neon sign radiating the name "Blue Oyster Bar."

Without any attentiveness, both girls cross the street following the music and end up at a well lit staircase with a black and white sign reading "All GI's Welcome." It's a long straight flight of steps, and Jilly signals this must be a safe quiet place. Mia agrees with the comment, "How bad can it be if they play The Beatles." As they reach the top of the staircase, they have a clear view of a low lit bar surrounded by twenty tables. Each of the tables has a small lighted candle glowing which gives the Blue Oyster Bar a strange, but romantic feeling. The girls decide to sit at the bar instead of a table. The bartender speaks English, but with a French accent and asks the girls what would they like to order. Jilly wants something sweet and potent and orders a Zombie while Mia orders a hot tea since she doesn't want to reawaken her ills.

Deliberating the correct strategy to use when writing to Ricky and George is interrupted by the sucking sound of Jilly's straw sipping up the last few drops left in her Zombie. Unannounced the bartender brings over two more drinks and signals that the gentleman sitting at the other end of the bar is buying. The girls immediately wave off the drinks, but the bartender is persistent. Both girls thank the man who is a noticeably well-dressed Vietnamese man with slicked back jet black hair with a light gray streak running from his forehead to the rear of his scalp. The mystery man walks toward the girls and introduces himself as Lanh Phu which means "good, favorable, gentle" in Vietnamese.

Mia is in no mood for talking to a stranger and recalls the warnings from Betty Santos. She politely lets Lanh know they both need to be left alone, but Lanh is relentless in his approach and just continues to inject himself into the girls' conversation. Jilly also begins to get uncomfortable vibes and excuses Mia and herself to leave for the ladies' room. As the girls step away, the bartender points the way to the ladies' room. Waiting for the girls to be out of site, Lanh immediately cups both his hands over the girls' drinks.

In the ladies' room, their conversation unwillingly is now forced to be how to get rid of Lanh instead of discussing a plan for their husbands. Mia suggests that they go back to the bar, gulp down their drinks, tell Lanh they must go, leave the Blue Oyster and return to the Red Cross. With both in agreement, the girls return to the bar and take their same seats while Mia speaks first. She tells Lanh that the Red Cross curfew is 11 pm, and they must leave since they have only fifteen minutes left to get back. Both girls guzzle down the two drinks and say goodbye to Lanh. They quickly walk down the stairs and turn right on Tù Do Street. About half way down the street, Mia turns around to see if they are free and clear. With no sign of Lanh anywhere, the girls feel as though it's finally safe to slow down to a normal pace.

The short walk back now seems much longer. With the glare of night lights now hurting their eyes, a woozy feeling takes over both young, vibrant bodies. The street noise strokes them into a headache, and their ears begin to throb while their bodies profusely perspire. Mia reaches out to Jilly, both now only seeing shadows in place of images, and they tightly embrace. Jilly spits out the words "We've been drugged!" Each slowly falls to their knees on the sidewalk in a shadowed area. Without anyone around to witness what was happening, a feeling of terror overcomes Mia and Jilly. Speaking becomes just a slurring sound, and the two sets of eyes begin to close. Two shadows in the night appear and approach the girls. Lifting them off the sidewalk, they are carried to a nearby waiting van. Quietly and swiftly, the girls are laid down in the cargo area of the van, covered with blankets, and rapidly disappear into the night lights of Saigon. The seizure was so well timed and orchestrated that no one even noticed. With military type precision in a blink of an eye, Mia and Jilly are professionally kidnapped and absorbed into the underground world of a war.

The sun is peeking through a crack in the small hut, its light waves are radiating on Jilly's face, waking her up to realize her mouth is gagged, hands and feet bound together. A full view gives Jilly the sad fact that both her and Mia are tightly secured by a chain to a steel pole that's anchored into the ground. Jilly's quick visual inspection of their surroundings displays nothing but four walls and a hard dirt floor to lay on. Their mouths are filled with cloth and taped closed so yelling for help is not an option.

Brash sounds of a group of men arguing in Vietnamese suddenly wakes Mia as her eyes open for the first time since the doping incident. Sun streaks are now making Mia's vision hard to properly focus, and both girls are still woozy. The arguing noise from outside abruptly fades into silence with a new sound of a vehicle ignition starting and wheels in motion pulling away. Jilly and Mia can only communicate between each other by humming or blinking their eyes. Disturbing thoughts now run through their minds. They have no idea why they were taken or where they are. As frightening as it was to be kidnapped, the girls are now about to meet their new enslaved leader as the hut door quickly opens. At first glance, both girls immediately gasp when a middle age Vietnamese man appears wearing a large weaved bamboo coolie hat with a chin cord. Coolie hats resemble upside down cones and are commonly worn by Vietnam farmers to help keep the sun off their heads and shoulders. He appears to have only two upper teeth when he opens his mouth and has a jagged four-inch scar on his right cheek. He is wearing mud stained Vietnamese pajama-like farmer clothes which are tied by rope around his thin waist. On his filthy dirty feet are worn out handmade sandals which are constructed out of used car tires laced with rubber strips.

An empty bucket and two bowls, one with rice and the other water, are slid on the dirt floor between the girls. Their captor yells out something in Vietnamese and begins to remove their bindings except for the chains around their ankles. The captor yells out another crazy sounding remark and leaves Mia and Jilly alone to whimper as they give each other a passionate embrace. Gazing into each other's eyes, the two share their feelings about how difficult it will be from here on in. The girls are hungry, and together they fumble trying to grasp the bowl of rice with one of their hands while using the other hand as a utensil to eat the rice. The wooden bowl is old and dirty helping to make the rice appear like it is sprinkled with small dead insects. Their hunger attempts to overcome what they are looking at and forces them to begin eating. The unexpected crunchiness of the rice causes them to gag on their first mouth full. Trying to swallow the rice is very difficult and is repeatedly followed by vomiting. They try to wash away the bad taste by sharing a bowl of murky water. Staring at the battered wooden bucket, Mia guesses that it must be used as a toilet, and Jilly agrees with a yes gesture. Wishing and wanting a simple thing as a bath or even the use of a washcloth and soap is only a remote dream.

Smelling their own body odor as they sit in filth is demoralizing and only further breaks down what's left of their human decency. Their clothes are torn and stained with their own blood prompted by small cuts and abrasions. At this point, Mia and Jilly realize they don't have any shoes, and their feet are ripped and torn with scrapes from being dragged by their kidnappers. Jilly feels her hair, and it feels wet and oily, and Mia realizes her own hair is blood stained and muddy.

Jilly cries uncontrollably and softly whimpers how much she misses George, Mom, Dad, and Ali. Mia, already filled with her own tears, also whimpers Ricky's name and asks if Jilly believes in God. Her response, "Why is He letting this happen to us" surprises Mia, and she replies, "Everything God does has a purpose."

As night falls, they softly begin to sing Beatles songs to calm their fears of the unknown. Whispering the lyrics so their captors wouldn't hear them, the simple melodies provided them sustenance to imagine they were in a much better place. During the night, they begin to envision Ricky and George lying next to them, hearing their soothing words of comfort that all will be okay.

The visions place them into a mental state which helps diminish their overwhelming fears. They allow the girls the capability to fall asleep in peace. In the darkness of a long, arduous night, the lyrics of "In My life" offer Mia and Jilly with a completely new meaning, one which may not mean a happy ending.

Mia and Jilly begin to comprehend the fault in their own strong will which blinded them to make irrational decisions concerning their safety. Each girl is now broken by the fact that they should have paid more attention to all the warning signs which were given to them by their husbands, friends, family, and donut dollies. They now know they should have stayed in Fairfield. Wishing and hoping that they would somehow be rescued is becoming a distant dream. Together each girl realizes their predicament is much bigger than they are or anyone ever would have imagined. Unanswered prayers lead them to believe it may now be hopeless. Reoccurring nightmares reflect images that their treatment will only become worse.

Only the lonely will perish, but they realize they still have each other; companionship will keep them alive. What seemed like an eternity, but only a week later, the girls are once again awaken by the familiar sound of men arguing outside the hut. But this time it's much different. The hut door hurriedly opens as the panting of the girls reaches new levels. Four strange Vietnamese men burst through the doorway and start binding them once again. Mia and Jilly are dragged out, while humming for help, to the same waiting van and dumped like garbage onto the van floor next to a pile of dead fish. They are again covered with a blanket to hide them from any onlookers. The ride is bumpy and winding, and the driver seems to be in a rush to arrive to his destination. The van has a strong putrid smell of foul fish thus giving the girls another sign that the end must be near, and their lives will be over soon.

A short time later, the van comes to a stop and very quickly the sliding door of the van opens. The girls are crudely man-handled and dragged on the ground to a pier on the water's edge. It appears to the girls to be a fishing marina on a river. Hanging over the water are two large bamboo cages hung by rope on pulleys. The gang of four slowly yank on the rope bringing down the cages to the deck of the pier. The river is muddy brown in color, rendering zero visibility. Nothing can be seen laying in or under the murky waters.

The girls are unbound by one of the captors. At knife point they are ordered to enter separate bamboo cages as each door is opened. Another captor wraps a short-looped metal cable around each cage door with padlocks. Two captors at each line of rope grab the rope by pulling hard to raise the two cages up to their perches. The lines are then tied off with bowline knots to the nearest piling. In a flash without Jilly or Mia knowing what is going on, they are now dangling in midair like caged animals.

The terror in the girl's minds now reaches a new plateau. Being trapped in a cage in the murky river brings unimaginable fears. Once they were placed in their cages, Mia and Jilly grab tightly onto the bamboo bars trying to jiggle something loose, but the cages are well constructed and don't budge. The hot sun beats down on their heads and backs. They are hunched over, cramped while feeling the dense heat and humidity. The close-up impression of the muddy river brings a distant memory back to Mia, recalling when she was a young girl. Every few years, the Mississippi River would run over its banks causing a flood stage, washing away the fertile farm soil of southern Illinois. However, the water color of the My Tho River was a dark cocoa brown versus the pale brown of the Mississippi. Mia and Jilly can at least see each other when hanging in the cages, and it is some sort of small consolation helping them calm some fears.

During most nights, the Viet Cong would take Mia and Jilly out of the water to one of the larger huts where they were repeatedly beaten and raped at knife point. Moving the girls to a hut at night gave the Viet Cong the ability to do whatever they wanted without running the fear of being heard or seen. To help keep the girls from fighting back, the Viet Cong injected them with heroin. With no one around to hear their cries for help, the screaming and resistance began to diminish. Some of the Viet Cong would lie next to the girls during the night until morning. The heroin soon takes complete control over their willingness to resist, and the girls submit to becoming sex slaves to the Viet Cong. Jilly and Mia were now only able to stare with a glance at each other while being raped. By using only their eyes, they can communicate and express the suffering without speaking a word. Mia and Jilly begin to wish and hope the suffering can come to a quick end, even though it may mean death. They are now both in a zombie state at the gates of hell.

Chapter 7

1968 South Vietnam

A dark cloud of true fear begins to engulf the lives of Ricky and George leaving them with little known options. Their true fear begins to perceive the forces of danger causing them to experience a change in their own human behavior. Helplessness is now a feeling they will get to know well.

George and Ricky are worried and perplexed by the returned letters they sent. They opt out using the Military Affiliated Radio Service (MARS) which was available to them to place calls back home because it was hard to do. The waiting list to call back home was too long, and the time limit restrictions were too cumbersome. Instead they agreed that they needed to rush the calls because they must have unlimited time to complete their calls.

During the Vietnam conflict, there were no individual personal cellular or landline telephones available for soldiers or sailors to use for calling family members back home. To address this, United States MARS (Military Affiliate Radio Service) stations from all branches of the service, Army, Navy, Marines, and Air Force, were deployed throughout Vietnam. The MARS system offered soldiers and sailors a way to personally communicate with loved ones back home via the use of a "phone-patch" telephone connection over short-wave radio. MARS stations would allow each soldier a free five minute personal radio telephone call home to the United States. In just about all cases, MARS was the only way soldiers could call home without paying a fortune. In other words, "MARS was the Soldiers' Free Telephone Company." The reality was that the current list to call home from Tan Son Nhut Air Base and the surrounding two other area bases had over 2,000 servicemen's names posted. Ninety-nine percent of servicemen never got the chance to use the MARS system because of its stringent limitations. Most tours of duty were over, and soldiers never had a chance to ever call home under the MARS system.

Ricky and George decided to visit an AT&T office in Saigon to place international phone calls back home. Their first call is to the Fairfield apartment of Jilly and Mia which doesn't go through due to a recording stating the number has been disconnected. George, filled with anger, slams the phone down so hard the AT&T agent hears the bang. Ricky waves him off with an apologetic gesture. Another call is immediately placed, but this time to Jilly's mother, Edith, in Peshtigo. Ringing for many unanswered seconds, George is almost ready to give up when suddenly Edith picks up the phone with a sorrowful hello. Just the sound of hearing George's voice makes Edith feel faint. She has been experiencing an unrestful feeling for several days. In a very low tone of voice, Edith says, "I was waiting for this call. I have been having terrible nightmares about Jilly and Mia." Edith asks, "Is something wrong?"

George says, "I have some bad news. Jilly and Mia are missing."

During his conversation with Edith, George realizes that the girls deliberately planned their transfer to Vietnam against his and Ricky's wishes. Edith unknowingly has now let the girls' secret out into the open, and she is very distressed by the news. For the past few days, Edith has been having nightmares, and in each case, they involve Jilly and Mia. In her dreams, she sees a group of men dressed in assumed ninja type robes with ropes tied around their waists chasing the girls. In each reoccurring dream, Edith never sees the faces of who the girls are running from, but assumes they are Asian. She hears Jilly and Mia screaming for help in every dream. As she searches for them, the screams always seem to fade into the distance just before she awakes. The dreams seem so real to Edith that when she awakes, her heart is beating rapidly, and she's in a cold sweat.

George tries to calm Edith's fears by promising her that they will find the girls. He ends the call by telling her, "Mom, Ricky and I will find where they are and have them call you immediately." Ali comes from the kitchen realizing Edith is upset and asks, "Don't tell me something has happen to Jilly and Mia."

Edith ends the conversation with Ricky by saying, "I pray to God you find them, please find them," and hangs up.

Ali now wants to know what has happened after Edith tells her that Jilly and Mia never told George or Ricky they were going to Vietnam. With tears running down her face, Edith cries out, "They are missing," which ignites Ali to breakdown in tears. Ali says, "It's so hard to believe this! I feel like I'm in the middle of a nightmare!" Ali hugs her mother and says, "I hope and pray they will find them, Mom."

George and Ricky are fit to be tied, but at the same time are lost for words. "How could they do this to us? They refused to pay attention to our warnings," shouts Ricky. "What were they thinking?" Another phone call is placed to Travis, and Ricky speaks to one of the buddies who moved the girls. A disappointed Ricky shakes his head in disgust when he hears of the promised secrets given by his friends. George punches the sheetrock wall with his fist breaking through. Frustration takes over both men along with the ever-present thought of helplessness. Their minds are now speeding in forward motion thinking that something evil might have happened to the girls. Terror and panic is blocking their trained military thought process. Ricky cries out loud, "We should have made sure they listened to us! Why didn't they listen? Where could they be? Why are they not in touch with anyone? What are we going to do?" Danger, danger, danger echoes over and over in their minds.

Continuing to try hard to back track the girls' whereabouts, reaching out to the American Red Cross office in Fairfield becomes the next step. Before the call is placed, George walks down the hall and walks over to the AT&T office manager. He admits to the manager that he punched a hole in the wall because he had just found their wives were missing. The manager asks to be shown the damage and as they both walk down the hall, George mentions that he wants to pay for the damage. When they reach the small closet-type phone room where Ricky is sitting and waiting, George points to the damaged area. The manager realizes that both men were probably in the military and asks where they are stationed. When the AT&T manager is told Tan Son Nhut Air Base he cannot help but notice the panicked look on both the mens' faces.

Ricky explains that they had just discovered their wives were missing and apologizes for the damage. George tells the manager that a few more calls need to be made by them, and they are hopeful this may all be a big misunderstanding. The AT&T manager expresses concern about their wives and suggests they finish their calls and see him in his office before they leave. He reminds them to please try to refrain from any further bursts of anger.

Ricky thinks it is best for him to handle the next call to the Red Cross in Fairfield. While being transferred from one person to another, anger once again begins to creep up on Ricky. George places his hand on Ricky's shoulder for some added support to calm him down. The bad news continues as it is revealed during the call that the girls were in fact transferred to Saigon. The guys realize that the Red Cross facility in Saigon is only a few blocks away from where they were. George finally places the last call to Jilly's mom, Edith, to let her know what they have found out. The conversation with Edith was gloomy. Edith expressed to George that she felt as though she had already lived this nightmare in the dreams she had been having. Edith's inner self was hoping for the best, but she was resistant to feel relieved by the news. A feeling of living in a surreal world takes over as Edith tries to comprehend telling her husband, Dave, what has happened. She admits to herself that the future looks gloomy and will not give her the miracle she yearns for.

Before leaving AT&T, they stop by the manager's office with a hurried look on their faces. They were told not to worry about the cost to repair the damage. The manager wished them the best of luck in finding their wives and closes off with, "I'm sure it will all work out."

Supported by fear, George and Ricky quickly begin their walk to the Red Cross building. Their walk quickly turns into a jog as they realize every second may be the difference between life and death. When the Red Cross building is within sight, running the rest of the way becomes an instinct for both men. Reaching the front steps of the Red Cross building, completely out of breath, Ricky forcefully pushes open the wooden double doors. As the guys rush in, they are herded to an arrival desk where they both state the purpose of their visit. The receptionist dials the nurse manager, Betty Santos, who informs the receptionist she will be down in a minute. George and Ricky are told to take a seat, and someone will be with them shortly.

Commotion breaks out while the guys are patiently waiting, and Ricky walks back to the receptionist to ask what's going on. It's explained that many wounded soldiers will immediately be flown into local hospitals, and every available medical person is now on stand-by emergency call. Instead of a few minutes, it's now about an hour and still no one has come to see the eager men. Just as George gets up to walk toward the receptionist, they hear their names being called by Betty Santos. She apologizes for her lateness and states, "Things are getting crazy around here lately."

Betty Santos guides both men into an unoccupied office down the hallway where Ricky and George are asked to take a seat. Betty sits behind a desk while the guys pull up two metal upholstered side chairs. Ricky starts off advising Betty that their wives have come to Vietnam without their approval. Also the fact that their wives have been traced to the Red Cross in Saigon poses a desperate hope that they can be found. Betty Santos voices her surprise to hear that the girls were married, and they did in fact report to her about three weeks ago. Betty says, "The girls' paperwork never revealed any mention of them being married." Ricky advises Betty that their wives only used their maiden names. Betty nods her head, then gives them the bad news that the girls left the building without ever properly signing out, while explaining it was an important rule to follow. George breaks in by saying, "Now that sounds like our wives." Betty continues with another bit of bad news with the fact that the girls have been marked AWOL (absent without leave) ever since. Betty strongly suggests that both men visit Police Headquarters and speak to Detective Chi, since the Red Cross has already done so, by reporting them missing after the first forty-eight hours. With tears in her eyes and a lump in her throat, Betty slowly writes down the Police Headquarters address and Detective Chi's phone number while mentioning that the detective speaks English.

It's now the middle of day with traffic congestion, loud noise, and the hustle-bustle of Saigon's city life on full display. Once outside the Red Cross building, Ricky hails a cab and shows the note from Betty Santos to the driver who remarks "Okay, Joe." The ride seems to go very slow as countless bicycles and shooters are disobeying the traffic signals and causing a backup at each intersection. George mentions to Ricky, "We could have been walking faster than this damn taxi." When they finally arrive, Ricky and George rushed into Police Headquarters and announced their request to see Detective Chi. Between the frustrating taxi ride, long distance calls, and not finding out the whereabouts of Mia and Jilly are finally making their frustrations show up in bursts of anger. George and Ricky now realize that they really are angry at themselves for allowing this to go as far as it did. This entire frustrating calamity brings the two men to realize that they never really knew the two women they married. Witnessing some of the warning signs in their relationships with Mia and Jilly should have never been brushed aside. George and Ricky wish to themselves if only they could go back in time when at Frisco's Restaurant in Fairfield.

They are motioned by a uniformed police officer to take a seat and wait for Detective Chi. George says to Ricky, "This is just like the Air Force. Hurry up and wait," as both guys sit and wait. Consistently looking at their watches every few seconds, Ricky and George are getting more frustrated by the second. It seems like time was rushing by, but it was only a ten minute wait. Detective Chi appears and walks over to Ricky and George to introduce himself. The two men are instructed by Chi to follow him into his office. All three take seats with Chi behind his desk. There are piles of files scatted all over his desk and cabinets behind him. Chi's wrinkled face, receding hair line, and thick steel rim glasses perched above his nostrils reveals the fact that he is fast approaching retirement. The detective explains that he has just received a call from nurse Santos and has been brought up to date concerning two missing American Red Cross nurses. Chi's first question is, "When was the last time you saw your wives?"

George tells Chi, "It was on March 5th when we left Travis Air Force Base for Vietnam."

Chi replies, "Have any of you spoken to Mia or Jilly since March 5th?"

Ricky answers, "No, sir." Chi explains that his office will work hard to find Mia and Jilly, but reluctantly mentions that since the Tet Offensive there have been hundreds of missing persons in the city of Saigon. Ricky's anger is echoing in his head. Speaking out in a burst of anger, he says, "We should have never been married before our tour of duty! Mia and Jilly never would have followed us to Vietnam if we weren't married." George gives Ricky a look of support and nods his head yes as both men reach their highest degree of fear.

Chi points to all the piles of folders in front and around him. Reaching out to grab a bunch of files, Chi reads out loud a few case files. "This one involves a three-year-old girl who was reported missing when her mother left her alone for a moment so she could run out to buy some vegetables. Another reports a van stopping in the street to grab a thirteen-year-old girl and speeds away." Adding a third case, Chi says, "This one is a report of a husband and wife being taken in broad daylight while their entire family watched."

Chi believes that this case deserves priority since it involves two American women associated with the military. This leads Chi to believe there is a deviant motive which may be out of his realm of authority. Ricky and George are reluctantly thankful for Chi's candor and willingness to give their missing wives some sort of priority. George writes down their base phone number and extensions and hands it over to Chi. Chi bows and extends his hand to George and Ricky saying, "I'll do my best to find your wives."

Now filled with nothing but true fear, Ricky and George return by cab to Tan Son Nhut Air Base and walk directly to their commanding officer Colonel Shaw's office to discuss their dilemma. George and Ricky have the highest respect for their commanding officer. Colonel Shaw has chosen the Air Force as a career after serving in WWII in the Army Air Corps, working his way up through the ranks starting as an enlisted man. The Colonel reached the rank of master sergeant, then transferred to Officers Training School in 1956, finally graduating from the Air Force Academy in 1960. Shaw's Vietnam service includes three tours of duty, and he knows his way around the country and its people. Shaw also speaks Vietnamese very well and has many old friends in Saigon.

After hearing the horrible news about their missing wives, Colonel Shaw recommends they hire a private investigator, and he will provide the name of a man he trusts. He asks George and Ricky to allow him to make a few phone calls himself to former Army intelligence contacts to see what he can find out. Colonel Shaw describes in detail to the men about a vibrant underground criminal element operating in Saigon ever since the war began. Ricky and George stand numb when they hear Shaw give some of the details kidnapers use. It is clearly pointed out by Colonel Shaw that both men can't trust the police department because of all the corruption. Colonel Shaw reminds them to stop by his office in the morning for the private investigator's name. The Colonel also recommends that they put in a special request for a leave of absence, which he will sign off on and approve. The time off will be a great help to Ricky and George during their investigation of finding their wives. Both men thank the Colonel for his input and exit his office feeling a bit better than when they spoke to the Detective Chi.

The next morning, Ricky and George report to Colonel Shaw's office to pick up the name of the private investigator. The Colonel hand wrote the name of Vinh Phan and his phone number. Before leaving the Colonel's office, Ricky and George fill out and hand in their requests for taking one week leave of absence. Returning to their barracks without looking or speaking to each other is so noticeable that fellow officers sense that something bad is brewing. All further conversations between Ricky and George turn to explosive thoughts of what might have happened to their wives. Their subconscious minds are simultaneously thinking about the horrible acts their wives may be going through. During the night, Ricky and George can't sleep just thinking about their wives. Trembling fears keep them on the brink of tears while each doesn't want to show his sadness to the other. The men look at their watches all through the night hoping the night will soon pass so their searching for Mia and Jilly can truly begin.

The next day they are notified that their papers for special leave have been approved and are waiting for them to be picked up. George suggests they eat something first on base before heading to the Colonel's office, and Ricky agrees. The Chow Hall is nothing but a large sheet metal pole building which is separated into two sections, one for "Enlisted Men" and the other for "Officers."

Pole building design was pioneered in the 1930's in the United States originally using utility poles for horse barns and agricultural buildings. The depressed value of agricultural products in the 1920's and 1930's and the emergence of large, corporate farming in the 1930's created a demand for larger, cheaper agricultural buildings. As the practice took hold, rather than using utility poles, materials such as pole barn nails were developed specifically for this type of construction, making the process more affordable and reliable. Most of the construction of air bases in the Vietnam War were constructed by the US Navy (Construction Battalion) commonly known as the Navy Seabees.

The techniques used in the construction of pole buildings made a quick and economical method of adding outbuildings and a natural for military use in The Vietnam War. Around North America, numerous pole built structures are still readily seen in rural and industrial areas, for the galvanized steel siding and roofing of the thirties has proven to be very durable and able to withstand years of high winds, snow, and ice storms.

George is the hungriest of the two as Ricky is distracted and still in disbelief. They grab a metal tray and walk the line as hot food is being served. George ends up with heaping portions of scrambled eggs, fried spam, hominy grits, and toast. Ricky has only a bowl of Kellogg's Rice Krispies and milk.

A familiar warning siren suddenly sounds which alarms all base personnel the signal to take cover. George quickly stands up, ready to head for the nearest bunker and realizes that Ricky is in no mood to move. Mortar explosions begin to rumble in the near distance and are getting closer by the second. Ricky, as though in a trance, does not respond when George yells, "Let's go, Ricky!" George grabs Ricky under his arms from behind and lifts him with brute force. Dragging Ricky almost ten feet, Ricky finally awakens from his trance and begins to realize what is happening. Just as the two buddies reach the doorway, there is a sharp sounding explosion. The explosion creates a small crater destroying the entire front of the building. Within a split second, the explosion erases the lives of Ricky, George, and six other servicemen. When the dust and smoke settles, all the hopes and dreams of two men who only wanted to love their wives are ripped apart and buried by ashes and debris. Once again the war takes its toll on non-combat support personnel. The screams and yells of recovery crews echo across the base searching for survivors.

Ripping through the rubble, the rescue crew try desperately to find survivors. The debris is scatted everywhere and doesn't make the searching effort an easy mission. Ragged and ripped pieces of sheet metal acting like shrapnel have cut through human flesh like sharp swords. The fears and uncertainties of the rescuers are confirmed when eight bodies showing signs of dismemberment are uncovered. Unfortunately, Ricky and George's lives were tragically cut short and the love for their wives died along with them. The sounds of silence now tell the story of two men who were both rich in their own way. Being innocent victims, Ricky and George were only guilty of loving their wives, and that same love also died along with them.

Chapter 8

2005 South Vietnam

War sometimes acts as a double-edged sword, on one side it causes death and destruction and on the other side it forces change for the good to occur. Transformation moves slowly over time and with that change comes a recovering society which offers its people more liberties and the pursuit of happiness.

Chet immediately notices that the town of Tra Vinh has drastically changed over the years. The former small village is now a bustling manufacturing zone utilizing its number one asset, The My Tho River, strategically to ship its finished goods to market. Missing are the old "Junk Boats" that once smuggled supplies to the Viet Cong. These boats have now been replaced by small barges and powered vessels trolling freely up and down the river. Ta suggests that they board a small power boat which will give them a better view to inspect their surroundings. The murky brown color of the river hasn't changed much in almost forty years. Chet wonders what the area would look like if the war had never happened. Despite all the negatives Chet heard about Vietnam because of the war, he firmly believes the people of Vietnam are now better off than ever before.

"What did you witness that was so startling it has lived with you for all these years," asks Chet. Ta begins an explanation which he knows will not register well with Chet, but feels the story must be told for the sake of the two innocent women connected spiritually to him through his dreams. The five horsepower Suzuki engine cuts its way quietly through the murky water with ease. Slowly moving through the same water with the mild wind in his face reminds Chet of time on PCF-33. He feels a sense of accomplishment having the ability to return to Vietnam during a peaceful time. He is proud that this trip to the land he once roamed as a fighting gunner's mate is now so vibrant.

Ta continues to pick up his harrowing story of when PCF-33 pulled into the old marina. The Viet Cong felt that they would be caught red-handed if the swift boat sailors saw the women hanging in cages. So that's when the leader of the Viet Cong ordered the cages dropped into the water. The women were given a two-foot-long hollowed out bamboo pole each to use as snorkels for breathing. The women were both crying and screaming as they were hurriedly being lowered into the water. This immediately stopped as the cages were completed submerged under the brown murky water. By the time PCF-33 pulled into the dock of the old marina, the cages were completely out of sight, and the women were under water. Ta went on to describe the shaking fear he felt witnessing what happened and described the haunting sound of the big brown dog. He remembers the dog wanting to jump into the water, but one of the crew held him back on a leash. That's when the Viet Cong heard him moving around, hidden in the bush. Once he realized he was spotted, Ta began to run as fast as he could to get away. As young Ta reached the main hut, he saw the sun reflecting off a shiny object. He quickly bent over and picked up the object and continued to run like a bat out of hell to safety.

Remembering the winds rapidly turn into gale-force, Ta recalled PCF-33 leaving the old marina, moving back down river towards very heavy seas. Chet asks what happened to the women in the cages, and what was shining in the light?

Ta sadly relays to Chet that the Viet Cong heeded PCF-33's warning and ran for higher ground, thus leaving the girls caged underwater with only their short bamboo snorkel poles. As the typhoon moved rapidly into a normally tranquil river, the waters quickly turned into raging waves. A fifteen-foot tidal surge blew into the river, destroying everything in its path. The strong storm force washed away every part of the old marina, including the cages which held Mia and Jilly. Chet cries out, "Oh, my God, what did we do!" thinking that he and his crew were responsible for the girls' deaths.

Ta's replies, "You didn't do anything wrong; those girls would have been killed anyway." Assuring Chet that all the nighttime screams he heard coming from the girls couldn't have been related to anything good happening to them. Ta said, "They wouldn't have survived much longer no matter what you did or didn't do." Who knows how much longer they would have survived as captives. Feeling Chet's pain, Ta sensed it was now time for Chet to know what the shiny items were. He slowly pulled an envelope out of his pocket and handed it to Chet.

Completely bewildered Chet carefully opens the envelope he was just handed and pours its contents into the palm of his left hand. He is astonished to see two sets of dog tags and one white gold wedding band linked together on a silver beaded chain. Under closer examination, Chet realizes the dog tags are military type and the ring has the inscription "Forever my love, George." He is astonished to read the name on the first set of dog tags. The tag is inscribed with the name Mia Flynn. The other tag is inscribed with the name Jill Landry. Both dog tags have strange service numbers preceded by the letters ARC. Chet is not familiar with the "ARC" alpha prefix type of service numbers. He tells Ta that he pledges to find out who these women were and rightfully return the items to their families.

Now realizing that PCF-33 played an unknowingly key role in the girls' deaths, Chet begins to grip the feeling of guilt. For the first time in his life, Chet now has seen the effects of an unintended consequence and recalls blaming the US military for many such consequences of the war. Forty years after the fact doesn't make the guilt seem any easier to accept, and he vows to find out why these two women died and were forgotten.

Cruising along the banks of the river for an hour or so, Ta points out other changes that have taken place since 1968. The jungle growth is now much higher than Chet remembers and shows no effects of the "Agent Orange" which was sprayed on the river banks. In fact the jungle has grown to its fullest extent leaving no sign of intervention by any war. Chet remarks, "Mother Nature always has a way to heal itself." As they turn the boat around, Chet's sight is once again filled with an easterly view, but this time the skies are clear with a slight wind in his face. When they arrive at the dock to return the small boat, Chet steps ashore first, hands over some cash, and thanks the boat owner. The men take the short walk back to the rental car, and Chet volunteers to take the wheel.

During the drive back to Ho Chi Minh City, Chet is upset as he reflects how close he and the crew of PCF-33 were to preventing such a tragedy from ever happening. Was there anything that the crew should have picked up on? Should they have stepped ashore? Why didn't they inspect the old marina grounds? Is the strange gurgling sound he has been hearing related to this misfortune?

Ta takes over the driving when Chet begins to have severe stomach pains. They change seats while Chet takes a swig of Dr. Diem's potion. He closes his eyes and doses off into a semiconscious sleep. The thoughts of what he was just told keep racing in his mind. He imagines the pain and suffering those two women must have gone though. He reminiscences about the moment when PCF-33 received a radio message from base headquarters ordering them, "Stop what they were doing and return at once," The winds were blowing hard and the tide was rising fast. Buck was barking hard and loud about something nearby, which under normal conditions Rugby would have investigated. Chet recalls looking toward the eastern horizon viewing the blackest of black sky coming their way. He remembers seeing Lieutenant Horner shout out to the crew, "Let's get the hell out of here" as the veins in his neck popped out as though they were going to explode. Chet reaches back into his pocket and pulls out the dog tags and wedding band Ta gave him and begins to slowly rub the raised letters of both girls' names. Wiping the tears from his eyes, he realizes that he now has a new mission to complete. Hours later after their return, the glowing moon was shining its bright light. Chet stared into that light contemplating what he and Ta saw and talked about during their visit to Tra Vinh.

After a sporadic night's sleep, Ta and Chet plan a visit to the United States Embassy in Ho Chi Minh City to help them find out if Ta's story can be officially documented. In Chet's mind, Ta's story must mean something and should be a vital part of any official investigation. Chet is very appreciative that his friend Ta can accompany him, and the men feel a new solid bond between each other. The stomach pain in Chet's gut is again misbehaving, and he asks Ta to remind him after the embassy visit to drop by Dr. Diem's office for a refill of his potion. The wait time at the embassy is long and after a little more than two hours, Chet's name is finally called. Ta and Chet explain their story and show the evidence of dog tags and wedding band while asking for whatever help that may be available. An embassy coordinator asks to see the dog tags and wedding band and excuses himself from the room for a few minutes. When the coordinator returns after thirty minutes, he returns the tags and wedding band back to Chet.

The coordinator asks Chet when he will be returning to the United States and if his schedule will allow him to meet with someone at the US State Department in Washington, DC. He gladly offers his itinerary revealing that he will be leaving for the United States in six days. Ta is asked to sign an affidavit recounting the turn of events he witnessed at the old marina in 1968 as a teenager. Chet is against the embassy's request to hold onto the dog tags and wedding band. They finally settle on the embassy taking pictures of the items.

The coordinator informs Chet that the "ARC" prefix on the dog tags were issued to American Red Cross personnel during the Vietnam War.

History shows the first American Red Cross field director arrived in South Vietnam in February 1962. Red Cross assistance to the armed forces expanded rapidly as the number of American service personnel increased, especially after the introduction of combat troops in 1965. The number of Red Cross workers in Vietnam and support areas in Southeast Asia peaked at nearly 500 in the 1968-1969 period while American troop strength was at its height. The American Red Cross moved its personnel out of Vietnam when the United States withdrew its fighting forces in March 1973. For a time afterwards, the Red Cross used Bangkok, Thailand as the base for its reduced operations in the region. Throughout the time Red Cross workers were in Vietnam, they shared the hardships and dangers of war with the military personnel they were there to serve. Many American Red Cross staff members lost their lives in Vietnam, and many others were injured.

Chet's schedule fits in well with The State Department, and he is given instructions that he will be contacted by the Washington, D.C. Headquarters once he returns home. Chet writes down all his pertinent contact info in exchange for the State Department contact info name of Russell Shields should he need to speak to someone in D.C. prior to being contacted by the State Department. Chet and Ta are thanked for what they have discovered and are reassured they will soon have answers to all their questions.

Chet and Ta decide to return to the same bar at The Grand Hotel for a few drinks and something to eat. This made it a good time and place to say their farewells. The bartender remembers the two men and asks if they want the same drinks, and both signal yes. Chet is the first to raise his glass to make a toast, and Ta follows in motion. Clinking glasses confirms the respect each man has for the other. Ta thanks Chet for the opportunity to get the heavy burden off his chest. Chet salutes Ta as one person he is so fortunate to have met. There is no question in either of their minds that their meeting was created by and a result of a higher authority. There is no logical way to explain how the two of them found each other. Both men promise to keep in touch and not to make this their last face-to-face meeting. Ta hopes that Chet's state of health improves. When dinner is finished, the men stand and give each other respectful hugs while affectionately patting their backs. As Ta walks away and reaches the bar doorway, he turns around and salutes Chet and says, "Goodbye for now, my friend."

Engrossed with the thought of the loss of two innocent lives, Chet embarks on his long journey home. His guilt once again erupts as he hallucinates what would have happened if PCF-33 paid attention to Buck's barking and had docked at the old marina for inspection. What would have happened if Lt. Commander Horner had not insisted on returning to the base? He daydreams about walking the docks of the old marina and hearing the very same gurgling sounds as in his nightmares. This time in his dream, he walks over to the opposite dock when his attention is attracted to bubbles coming from the murky water with Buck jumping in the water. A light ray of sun reflects off an S hook holding a line of rope. Hanging directly over his head just above the bubbles are two blocks and tackles which are tied down with two tightly wound lines. Chet and Rugby stop for a few seconds realizing that the lines are holding something in the water. Yanking on the closest line, the two men are only able to pull the heavy weight just to the surface. He notices the bamboo cage and a naked woman holding just a short snorkel tube. When the woman's head is out of the murky water, she quickly gasps for fresh air, but her body is limp in complete exhaustion. Chet then yells out to the other crew members for help. The first to run over is Lt. Horner who grabs the line and pulls, giving Chet and Rugby the needed strength to lift the cage with its contents onto the dock. Horner yells for all hands to help pull the second cage from the water. To the surprise of the crew, a second naked woman is lifted out of the murky water.

Aircraft bells ringing out loud awaken Chet. The pilot announces that the flight is making its final approach to Charleston International Airport. Chet is shocked that his dream seemed so real in every detail. Only the two women's faces were not visible to him in his dream. Chet can't yet put faces on Mia and Jilly which makes him feel that much more determined to find out who they were. In Chet's mind, the casualties of the Vietnam War now have two more stories to add to the already written long list of names. Chet stops to think of the large number of over fifty eight thousand Americans killed during the Vietnam war, knowing only a very small amount were women. The lone thought of these two women receiving the honor and recognition that they deserve makes Chet more determined to find out the truth wherever it may lead him.

Feeling a little home sick, Chet cannot wait to get back home to familiar surroundings. Chet hopes the wait will not be too long before he receives a call from Russell Shields of the State Department. Chet is looking forward to continuing his search for the truth and hopes that the State Department will help him in finding it. In the meantime, Chet traveling half way around the world and back has made him homesick. He can't wait to get home and sleep in his own bed.

Finally returning to his Kiawah Island home, Chet catches up on the menial tasks of laundry, mail, and responding to his messages. He places calls to his children and their families updating them about his trip to Vietnam, although he does not provide the intimate details. Chet feels he wants to have the complete story before sharing the incident with his family. It felt especially good to speak with his daughter, Cathy, granddaughters, Amanda, Amy, and daughter-in-law, Ann. As each of them spoke to him, Chet's mind played tricks on him by envisioning their faces to be those of Mia and Jilly. After the phone call, Chet thanked God for allowing the most important women in his life to be such loving individuals. He was overcome by strong emotions knowing that his family will never experience anything close to what he was told happen by Ta. The robust desire to hug each member of his family pushes Chet to visit Morgantown and York. He hopes that spending time with his loved ones will help lessen the terrible thoughts in his head.

The ride to visit his family was quiet. Although it was raining hard with the shifting winds pushing the droplets on his windshield from side to side. Tree branches were bending, and there was nothing but winding roads ahead which afforded low visibility. Having all the time in the world while driving to see his family, Chet had a lot of time to imagine many different "what if" scenarios. He and Nancy made the drive to Morgantown and York many times, favoring back roads over ugly interstates. The countryside views of rolling hills with scattered dairy farms always seemed to please Nancy.

Cherishing the first site of the happy faces on his daughter Cathy, daughter-in-law, Ann, and granddaughters, Amy and Amanda, makes the trip more than worthwhile. Hugging his daughter and granddaughters while smelling their hair brings back memories of when they were babies. Hugging his daughter-in-law, Ann, makes him wonder to himself what if Mia and Jilly were alive today, how would they look. Chet loves his son, Chester, and grandson, Neil, just as much as the women in his life, but due to the horror, he envisions Mia and Jilly experienced before their death; considering the faces of his son and grandson doesn't make him feel the same sadness he feels when he looks into the eyes of the women in his life.

During his conversations with his family, he tries explaining the trip to Vietnam, but is very careful not to get into the gruesome details. In avoiding what he saw and knows, Chet begins to experience quick, unstable visions of what he imagines happened to Mia and Jilly. Chet's visions are unhinged in his mind making it appear he was in another place in time. The awkwardness of not being himself has now overcome the joy of visiting his family. Making an excuse, Chet feels that he doesn't want to lie to his family when being asked about some of the details of the trip. Chet rushes to say goodbye and heads back to Kiawah.

On the return drive home, Chet is inspired to have an imaginary conversation with Mia and Jilly. He speaks to them as though they are passengers in his car. Chet mutters, "You both have given me the strength to find out the truth." Chet digs deep into his mind to envision what the girls looked like. The absence of their actual looks doesn't seem to stop him from mentally filling in the voids even down to the clothes they wore. Mia is seated in the front passenger seat with Jilly sitting in the rear passenger side seat. Looking young, beautiful, and vibrant just as they looked the night in Saigon while walking into the Blue Oyster Bar. The girls open up to Chet as though he was a father and apologize for not letting their family and husbands know their intentions. Jilly admits her and Mia were too much in love to know the real evils of war. The girls express missing the chance to say their goodbyes, but most of all they miss the lost opportunity to have children and raise families. Mia's loss are the pains of being a mother, waking up in the middle of the night, caring for a sick child. Wiping off dirty faces, hearing the first word of "Mommy," seeing that little sparkle in their eyes and hearing, "I love you, Mommy." Jilly grieves over not being able to share with her husband the occasional pains of marriage and their love for each other. Mia feels deprived of witnessing her children evolve from being toddlers, to teenagers, and finally growing into young adults graduating from college. Jilly regrets the lost opportunity of experiencing all the special moments associated with a full, rich life.

Being a good listener, Chet waits for Jilly to finish her thoughts and tells the girls' he has their dog tags and one white gold wedding band. Pausing while thinking, Chet then asks why is there only one wedding band? Did both of you have a wedding band? The wedding band I have is inscribed "Forever my love, George." Mia quickly responds, "I didn't want those creeps to take my ring, so I pretended to throw it in the river, but I actually cupped it in my hand and swallowed it." Mia tells Chet it was the only thing she had left to protect, and she was willing to die for it.

Caught up in his imaginary conversation, Chet begins to veer off the road. Suddenly the sound of a car horn startles him, and he quickly straightens his driving direction. Although he realizes it was only a day dream, Chet stills takes a quick look to his passenger side and back seat. The daydream seemed so real; for a moment he felt as though Mia and Jilly were riding with him. As Chet reaches to turn on the radio, he feels two hands on his shoulders. Looking in the rearview mirror, Mia and Jilly once more appear. They are smiling at him while making him feel that they wanted him to know that they were with their husbands in a much better place now.

It's about 9 pm, and Chet has another good hour more of driving before he reaches home. He decides once he arrives home, he will call Ta and share his true-to-life dream about Mia and Jilly. Chet plans to make the call at midnight which is noon time in Saigon assuming this will allow Ta to be well into his daily routine. Once at home, Chet has plenty of time until midnight rolls around, so he makes himself relaxed in his favorite chair and pours himself a Jack Daniels on the rocks with a lemon twist. When they speak, Chet doesn't want Ta to think he may be suffering from a mental disorder since he has already admitted to Ta about the crazy gurgling sounds he sporadically hears. However, Chet does feel very comfortable confiding in Ta and expects him to understand.

Shortly after the stroke of midnight, Chet dials Ta's number from his land line phone. On the third ring Ta picks up and says, "Hello, my friend, I see you made it back home safely."

Chet replies, "Yes, I did, and thank you again for helping me find some answers."

Ta asks, "Is your government helping you?"

Chet says, "Yes, I have appointments in about a week or so." Their conversation moves along which makes Ta feel as though there is something on Chet's mind. When Ta asks, "Do you need me to do something?" Ta's question opens the door for Chet to gently explain his dream about Mia and Jilly. Ta listens to every one of Chet's words very diligently and when Chet is finished telling his story, Ta waits silently before saying anything. Ta responds by telling Chet that he needs to think and absorb what he just heard. Chet says, "Does anything new come to mind about the way the girls were treated? Can you go back and take a better look for the missing ring?"

Ta replies, "Yes, I can, but I have to think how I will go about it." Knowing that Ta is a man of his word, Chet is elated to hear his answer. Chet thanks Ta and wishes him luck in searching for the missing ring. Ta ends the call by saying, "Goodbye, my friend, I'll let you know what I find." When the call ends, Chet felt much better confirming his confidence in Ta's desire and ability to find something that may have been previously overlooked.

Chapter 9

2005 Washington, DC

Ten days after Chet arrived back in the U.S., Russell Shields of the United States State Department calls. Russell introduces himself and admits he is very happy that this case was given to him by his superiors. Russell is a former Army Ranger who proudly served two tours in Vietnam. During his second tour of duty, Russell was wounded and treated by Red Cross nurses in a makeshift medical outpost. He tells Chet that he owes his life to those nurses who stopped the bleeding when he was wounded so he could be transported by Huey helicopter to a Saigon Hospital. Chet informs Russell that he is also a veteran of the war and feels a special attachment to the girls that is so strong, it is now affecting his life. Chet confesses to Russell about constantly hearing gurgling sounds and dreaming day and night about events that took place over forty years ago. Chet strongly feels the sounds and nightmares must have some connection with the girls. Understanding that Russell may think he is going crazy, trying to offer a better summary, Russell stops him by saying, "Brother, we all share some sort of bad dreams."

Russell provides an important piece of missing information to Chet. He gives him the name of the 1968 nurse manager in Saigon. Her name is Betty

Santos. Betty is now retired and lives in Alexandria, VA. Russell has already spoken to Betty, and she is open to a call or visit from Chet to discuss Mia and Jilly. Russell gives Chet Betty's phone number. He replies that he'll call her as soon as their meeting is over.

The backgrounds of Mia and Jilly are outlined by Russell along with their living family members. The unhappy news that none of Mia's family members are living upsets Chet. Jilly, on the other hand, has a widowed sister, Ali Parker, who still lives in Peshtigo. Russell pauses as he informs Chet that both Mia and Jilly were only married a few months. Their husbands were killed on the same day at Tan Son Nhut Air base. Department of Defense (DOD) records show John Ricciardi who was Mia's husband and George Wilkerson, Jilly's husband, were killed by a mortar attack on July 24th, 1968. The records show it was three weeks after the girls went missing. Russell agrees to email Chet additional family information including phone numbers.

Russell advises Chet that an appointment has been made for the following Monday at 9:00 am with Ken Gallagher, an old buddy of Russell's, at the Department of Defense in Washington, D.C. Russell explains to Chet that the people in the Pentagon administer and monitor the names of those who were killed in all wars. Russell believes that the two nurses' names should be added to the Vietnam Women's Memorial on the grounds of the Vietnam Veteran's Memorial in Washington, D.C. Chet agrees with Russell's opinion. He promises that will be at the DOD on Monday to meet with Ken Gallagher. Russell asks Chet to keep him informed of his findings. Russell also gives Chet the authority to make family and professional contacts on behalf of the State Department. Russell reminds him to act as though Mia and Jilly were his own family members, to remain respectful always. Russell and Chet agree that these two women were special people whose stories need to be corrected and recorded in history.

Immediately after leaving Russell, Chet calls Jilly's sister, Ali, in Peshtigo and leaves a message briefly describing his purpose to speak with her without bringing up the full intention of his call. Chet does not want to upset Ali before he can speak with her directly. A few hours later, Chet gives Betty Santos a call. Betty picks up the phone on the second ring. She relays that she had been expecting the call since her conversation with Russell Shields. Betty's voice is shaky and broken as she attempts to hold her composure. Chet can tell that Betty is extremely upset. Her despair is palpable with long silent pauses and whimpers. Betty relays that it seems like only yesterday that it was 1968, and the girls were leaving the Red Cross building. She remembers taking pictures in the lobby of the girls for her photo scrapbook. When Chet hears this, his eyes light up with excitement knowing that she has pictures that were taken just before they went missing. Chet tells Betty that he will be in D.C. next Monday for a meeting with the Pentagon. Once he leaves the Pentagon, depending on traffic conditions, he could be at her home in approximately thirty minutes. He asks if it would be okay if they had a brief meeting at her home in the afternoon to view and discuss the photos. Betty agrees to the meeting, and the conversation ends with Chet expressing how grateful he is and that he is looking forward meeting her.

The following Monday, Chet gives his deposition and signs the mandated paperwork at the Pentagon with Ken Gallagher. This finally allows the wheels of progress to move forward toward honoring the two women. Chet is angered by the cold, bureaucratic process involved while attempting to honor these two very brave, innocent women. The government's lack of compassion during the questioning leads Chet to believe that the girls were just objects to the government and not two women who lost their lives while serving their country. Asking himself why does the government act so cold and emotionless, Chet has a hard time coming to grips with his answers. Chet vehemently feels the brutal treatment of two women seemed to be swept away in the wording of the official questions, which angered him to almost walk out. Chet's feelings are now at a boiling point as he tries to hold back the anger, but instead a little voice in his mind stops him from leaving, and he completes the cold interview process. He does this for the sake of honoring Mia and Jilly.

In Washington, D.C., city life goes on with streets jam packed with taxis and buses moving the masses. Traffic signals change in unison, pedestrians walk about, the hustle and bustle of Washington D.C. on a typical busy work day. Chet drives by countless monuments, shrines, and memorials on his way to Betty Santos's apartment in Alexandria. He makes a brief stop at the National Mall to take in the view of the Washington Monument. It is almost midday, and the sun is shimmering atop the massive reflecting pond. Chet looks to his left and takes in the Washington Monument, then to the right absorbing the Lincoln Memorial views. Just ahead he sees the line of visitors at the low-profile Vietnam Veteran's Memorial Wall. Chet has kept his distance from visiting the wall for all these years, but now accepts the burden it will place in his heart. Walking alongside the memorial very slowly, not too close to feel its vibes, but far enough to feel its pain. Chet acted as though the wall was electrified and was afraid to touch it.

Chet walks half way from the path to the wall, stops and kneels, facing one of the black marble panel. Closing his eyes, he reaches in his pocket for the dog tags and wedding band. He then folds his hands and recites to himself the Lord's Prayer. When he is finished, Chet opens his eyes and to his surprise, he sees a group of Veterans gathered around him with their heads also bowed in prayer. The group is comprised of men in suits, bikers in jeans and leather jackets, laborers in work clothes, and a police officer in uniform. Looking straight ahead he sees the reflection of the group bouncing off the wall and realizes he is not alone. The pain and suffering of a war long ago can be seen in each of their eyes. A volunteer US Park Service man wearing a bright yellow hat and yellow jacket stands close behind him, places his right hand on Chet's left shoulder and says, "Welcome home, my brother."

The sky above the Memorial was pale cornflower blue in color. Cumulous clouds hanging low made Chet's exit even more memorable. It all turned out to be a day he will never forget. Circling in his car around the Lincoln Memorial, Chet follows the signs to the Arlington Memorial Bridge and heads west over the Potomac River. Choosing to ride on the George Washington Parkway southbound gives Chet a memorable view of D.C. from the other side of the Potomac and while passing by Reagan Washington National Airport. Betty's apartment complex comes up quickly once he exits on to Duke Street. There are ten mid-size two-story buildings in a well-kept complex displaying walls of fully bloomed blue hydrangea and red/white begonias. Chet parks in front of building "C" where Betty lives, walks into the small lobby, and presses the button for apartment 9. Wondering where this visit will lead him and how Betty Santos will react leaves Chet feeling anxious. He is buzzed in and walks down the hallway where Betty is already standing in the doorway. Betty's years of life are slightly exposed in her face and her still trim figure. Her years of service in Vietnam as a head nurse stands out in her body language still radiating the impression she is in charge. She greets Chet with a handshake followed by a surprise hug.

Betty asks Chet to take a seat in the living room where he sits down on a green and off white striped plush upholstered wing back chair. Betty walks to the small open kitchen area and brings back a tray of coffee and homemade crumb cake. She pours Chet and herself some coffee and suggests he can make it his own way, but Chet prefers it black with no sugar. The crumb cake is already sliced so Betty takes a piece for Chet, one for herself, and places them on small plates. Chet thanks Betty for the coffee and opens the conversation with, "I don't know where to begin." Betty tells Chet that she has been fully brought up to speed by Russell Shields. She offers her assistance to help solve a mystery that has been haunting her for almost forty years. She admits to Chet the girls not returning to the Red Cross back in 1968 made no sense to her. It also made her worry that something awful happened to them. The hospital administrators were too quick to accept the simple option that the girls just returned home. The administrators felt no need to ask any further questions. Betty stares into Chet's eyes and says, "I told them those girls are in trouble, and they need our help." Betty prays that the truth be uncovered and the records corrected. Chet agrees and notices what looks like an old album lying on the coffee table labelled "Red Cross 1968." Chet points at the album and asks, "Are the pictures of Mia and Jilly in this album?"

The desire to place faces on the two women is so strong, Chet is shaking with anxiety. Betty lifts the heavy photo album and hands it over to Chet and says, "Let me introduce you to Mia Flynn and Jill Landry." The album has a yellow sticky note marking the page to open. Taking a deep breath, Chet opens the album to the marked page, and he finally sees with his own eyes two beautiful women standing arm in arm together wearing light colored blouses and dark colored skirts. Betty points to Mia first. She has red hair, blue eyes, and a light skin tone complexion. Jill is a brunette with green eyes and a medium tone skin complexion. Betty also then points out two separate photos of each girl showing off great, big, wide smiles. Silently Chet focuses on the facial characteristics of Mia and Jilly and fills in the missing pieces of the girls in his mind. His imaginary conversation with the girls now has a direct visual connection down to the clothing they wore. The faces and images of Mia and Jilly wearing those great, big smiles make Chet feel as though the girls are now a part of his family.

Chet feels as though he has deeply known the girls without ever meeting them. He tells Betty that if he had to describe them, they would have looked the same as in her photos. Betty goes into a detailed account as she recalls that day in 1968 when Mia and Jilly walked out of the Red Cross building not ever to be seen again. The fact that the Red Cross and local officials at that time considered them only AWOL instead of missing made their disappearance seem like it was just a common event. Through Betty's eyes, Chet could see that not giving the girls' disappearance the attention it deserved was a big disappointment. Betty made it clear that she never believed her superiors for a moment and constantly tried to open an investigation into their disappearance. It has been an indelible dark stain in her mind, and she is so happy that the record will now be rewritten even though the outcome is so very sad. When Betty compiled her photo albums, she was very meticulous about keeping all photo negatives stored in the rear of the album. Betty hands Chet an envelope and explains that she has already made larger cropped copies of all the photos for him. Chet asks Betty if she knew that their husbands were both killed only three weeks after the girls went missing. She shook her head no and said, "Oh, my God, it just gets worse!" Tears begin to stream down her cheeks, and Chet reaches over to hold her hand. Betty then said, "I remember meeting their husbands at the Red Cross building in Saigon when they were searching for the girls. I recall they were so good looking and full of vitality. It sadly comes back to me now making it seem that the flames of four vibrant lives were extinguished like birthday candles on a cake."

Chet vows, "I promise to have them both honored." While saying goodbye, Betty and Chet make direct eye contact with each other forging a unique mutual bond. The two feel the intense attraction of a new friendship by now having so much in common like most Vietnam Veterans have for each other.

The lonely, sentimental ride back to Kiawah Island gives Chet the opportunity to contemplate on his accomplishments. His goal in finding out the truth about what happened to Mia and Jilly seems to be now within reach. The I-95 southbound ride begins taking a mental toll on Chet when he is somewhere south of Petersburg, VA. Leaving behind the metropolis of the Washington/Baltimore corridor in his rear-view mirror, Chet decides to stop and clear his head. It is a little past 7:00 pm and hunger pains begin to remind him that he hasn't eaten anything since the early morning. The upcoming exit sign for Roanoke Rapids, NC answers his desire to stop since it was a common place that he and Nancy used when traveling back and forth to Maryland. Once exiting he heads west on US-158 bringing him into the downtown Roanoke Rapids. Chet only remembers the location of Nancy's favorite restaurant on Roanoke Avenue, but not the name. Making a right turn on Roanoke, he proceeds two blocks and on the left side Chet finally sees Cozy's Café's red and white neon lit sign. He remembers the very good food and service and the cleanliness, especially the restrooms. Nancy never used restrooms that were smelly or dirty and would hold it in until they found the proper place. He and Nancy would never stop at an interstate exit rest area, but instead travel to the much more pleasant downtown areas.

Cozy's was appropriately named since it was a cozy place serving old time southern dishes specializing in country ham, sweet potatoes, hushpuppies, and homemade rhubarb pie. Taking a seat at the counter, Chet orders the house special. While sipping his iced tea and lemonade (Arnold Palmer), Chet catches the reflection off the wall mirror of an older couple sitting in one of the booths behind him. The couple was well dressed except for the older man wearing a worn-out baseball cap. The couple looked as though they have been married for at least fifty years. Chet surmises that this may be a date night out for the senior couple, and he wonders what his life would now be like if Nancy hadn't passed. Staring once again at the wall mirror, Chet notices the old cap is faded red in color with yellow lettering on the front. The older man looks toward Chet allowing him to read the faded ball cap lettering "WWII US Marine Corps Veteran."

After completely clearing his plate, Chet takes note that the name of his waitress was Sally. He requests his check and when she returns, Chet asks Sally about the old couple behind him. Sally is happy to tell Chet that the couple comes to Cozy's for dinner every Monday night. She explains that Bob, the old man, never takes his old Marine Corps cap off, and no one in town pays no mind because he earned wearing the cap after being wounded in the Pacific War. Chet asks Sally to add their check total to his amount and tell Bob, "Thank you for his service." Sally reaches out for Chet's hand and tells him that he is a good man. Chet settles the bill with Sally and walks out the door. He takes a last glance at old Bob before walking to his car which is parked in front of Cozy's Café.

Chet takes his position behind the wheel of the car just as his cell phone rings from an unknown number. Saying hello, he hears Ali Parker say, "Hello, Chet, is this a good time to talk?" Ali begins the conversation by letting Chet know that she has already spoken to Russell Shields at the State Department. Chet feels extremely uneasy sharing his findings about her sister, Jilly, and Mia over the phone. He asks Ali if they could meet next week. Ali agrees, but asks Chet if it is okay for them to meet in Chicago since she will be working at a tradeshow in McCormick Place. Ali advises Chet that she will be staying at The Water Tower Hotel, and she is free to meet for dinner next Thursday night. Chet tells Ali he is very familiar with the hotel and asks if they can meet at 8:00 pm at the Grill Bar. Ali agrees and then relays to Chet that she is proud of him for what he is doing for her sisters, Jilly and Mia. As they say their goodbyes, Chet begins to realize that Ali just called Jilly and Mia her sisters. It seemed odd to him, but when they meet he hopes to find what she meant by sisters.

After ending his call with Ali, Chet places the key in the ignition. He looks up and notices the old couple who he saw in Cozy's walking in front of his vehicle. Lined up right in the center of his hood ornament, standing and holding a salute. is the old man Bob? Chet opens the car door and stands at attention and salutes Bob in return. Both men then slowly bring down their salutes and while not speaking a word, the two veterans of different wars understand the unspoken connection between them.

Chet decides to fly into Chicago's O'Hare International Airport the night before his meeting with Ali. He asks his cab driver to take the scenic route along Lake Michigan to The Water Tower Hotel. It is a vibrant starry night with the skyline of Chicago reflecting off the lake. During his working career, Chet has spent many weeks a year on the road, with the city of Chicago as his busiest destination. His major client was Illinois Tool Works (ITW), its headquarters was in Glenview, IL. ITW made him the most successful sales director at the company where he worked for over twenty years, Boyce Insurance Agency.

ITW was an international conglomerate with over 50,000 employees operating under many subsidiaries in over 50 countries around the world. ITW had a vast amount of companies which assisted in making Chet the insurance kingpin of Boyce. Chet also gained the know-how and knowledge of innumerable types of manufacturing processes and components. Chet spoke of his own working career as a "Big fish in a little pond." What made Chet so good at what he did was his ability to investigate situations before pulling the trigger. A trait that has come in very handy in his work and life experiences.

The Water Tower Hotel is a grand old relic with all the modern conveniences. The hotel's name was taken by its proximity to the famous Water Tower of Chicago. The Water Tower was one of only a few structures that survived the great Chicago Fire of 1871 which burned down the city for two straight days. The castle style tower now proudly stands as a national landmark. The limestone blocks are painted in bright white, reflecting sunshine in daylight while being lit at night, making it the epicenter of city life.

Walking up to the front desk of the Water Tower Hotel, Chet sees small wooden cubicle sills in which room keys are stored. It reminded Chet of the old European custom of using extremely large room keys that are not meant to carry on your person when leaving the hotel. The room keys are given to the desk clerk each time guests leave the hotel. This old key system is also used by the hotel to let them know when the hotel guests are not in their room by hanging the key on its sill. Chet plans to do some sightseeing in the morning and call some of his buddies at ITW. When he finally settles into his room, he orders room service for a snack and retires early to get a good night sleep. The window of Chet's hotel room has an easterly view of Lake Michigan, giving him a glimpse of darkness as it begins to fall on the city. The lights of the city are slowly popping on, reflecting off the calm Lake Michigan water while sailboats are returning to their marinas.

The next night, Chet doesn't realize the time and is running late. As he glances at his watch, he sees that it is 8:20 and he's already twenty minutes past his scheduled appointment with Ali. Pushing himself hard, rushing to shower and shave, Chet seems to fumble each time he handles his razor and toothbrush. The wait for the elevator seems longer than usual. He has mixed emotions, hoping the meeting with Ali goes well. Walking at an accelerated pace across the marble flooring of the lobby, Chet feels as though he is ice skating his way to meet with Ali.

The Grill Bar had a small trio performing, playing the smooth jazz songs of Dave Brubeck. Chet walks directly towards the bartender and quickly notices the only woman seated alone at the bar. She was a very attractive well-dressed woman who seemed to be about the right age for Ali. Chet walks up to her. Ali stood up as she notices him approaching in the bar mirror. Chet says, "Ali, I presume?"

She gave him a great big smile and replies in a loving voice, "Yes, Chet, it's me," Both seemed slightly awkward when standing so close together. When their eyes met, the only natural response was to hug each other. The hug was held for more than a normal first-time meeting would be. Holding the hug, Chet immediately caught a pleasant scent which gives him the sensation of sailing with a mild fresh sea breeze blowing in his face. Slowly unbracing their hug, they sit at the bar. The jazz trio begins to play "Take Five," one of Chet's all-time favorite Dave Brubeck songs. David Warren Brubeck was an American jazz pianist and composer, considered to be one of the foremost exponents of cool jazz. The song "Take Five" was written in the early 1950's and is considered a jazz classic by most experts.

As the music plays, Chet is reminded of his personal experience meeting Dave Brubeck in the year 2000. He and Nancy were vacationing in Sanibel, FL at a small, quaint group of cottages called The Seaside Inn. On their first morning in Sanibel, Nancy decided to skip breakfast and sleep in another hour. Chet was hungry, but first decided to take a short stroll along the Seaside Inn's Gulf of Mexico beach. It was a beautiful morning, and the beach was filled with washed up sea shells. Collecting sea shells was one of Nancy's favorite things to do while in Sanibel. Chet knew it and couldn't wait to tell her of the large amounts laying in the sand waiting to be picked when he returned to their room later. After fifteen or twenty minutes of strolling along the tranquil breaking surf, Chet decided to walk over to the breakfast cottage where the Seaside Inn offered free breakfast to its guests. There was a small line at the omelet station, and Chet took his place in line behind an older, tall, slender man. They began to have a conversation about how peaceful and quiet the island of Sanibel was when Chet suddenly realized he was talking to Dave Brubeck, the father of "cool jazz." Chet immediately stopped what he was doing while he was holding a dish in each of his hands and introduced himself to Mr. Brubeck. Chet placed the two dishes down on the serving table and put out his hand to shake the most famous jazz piano player/composer in history. Dave Brubeck asked Chet to just call him Dave, and they shook hands.

When their omelets were ready, Dave asked Chet to sit with him, and the offer made him feel as happy as winning the lottery. Chet said, "Yes, sir!" and followed Dave as he leads the way to a small table in the corner of the room. The conversation mostly covered Dave's stories and his getting his first chance to perform. Dave explained to Chet the reason why he was in Sanibel was to write his memoirs which were going to be published soon. Dave realizing that Chet was a real jazz fan went into his beginnings in Stockton, CA and meeting and performing with other great jazz performers. Dave described in detail his early career after he served under in the US Army with General Patton in Europe. After his enlistment, Dave formed one of the first racially integrated bands called The Dave Brubeck Trio and in 1949, made it The Dave Brubeck Quartet. Dave went on to mention some of the most famous musicians who played in his bands as Cal Tjader, Ron Crotty, and Paul Desmond, just to name a few.

Each morning for the entire week, Chet had the honor of Dave holding him a seat in the same corner of the room at breakfast. Chet realized that spending time with Dave was a once in a lifetime event. Chet has never forgotten the warm and friendly person Dave Brubeck was, and with those treasured memories, he considers himself very fortunate.

When the bartender approaches, Chet orders a Jack Daniels on the rocks with a lemon twist, and Ali orders another Cosmo straight up. Chet and Ali are handed menus, and the bartender precisely recites the dinner specials. While reading their menus, Chet mentions to Ali that The Grill Bar's specialty are sizzling steaks. Ali answers, "I can smell the steak and hear the sizzling from here."

Chet starts the conversation by saying, "How do I begin?" He finally opens the conversation by telling Ali that he feels as though Jilly and Mia are now part of his life. He wished his findings were more pleasant to share, but they are not. He gently begins to tell Ali about the girls' stories from hell as he tries to hold his composure. In Chet's explanation, each time he uses the words caged, tortured, black ants, Ali's visions of horror take over her emotions. Ali's reactions are filled with tears and trembling. Chet remarks, "If only I could relive that day of September 13th, 1968, things might have worked out a little differently."

Ali asks, "What do you mean? What happened on that day?"

Chet replies, "It was the day that Typhon Cobra hit the main land in South Vietnam causing a tidal surge that swept away your sisters." After a long pause of silence with her two hands holding her head up, Chet asks Ali, "Are you okay?" She is so upset, speaking is too difficult, and she can only mumble the words, "Now I know the real date of their deaths."

Chet realizes what he has just done by giving Ali the day her sisters died and asks, "What day did you think they died?"

Ali says, "My mom, dad, and I never accepted Jilly and Mia to not ever return home, and it wasn't until twelve years later in 1980 when I finally recognized it was time to accept the sad fact that they were never coming home." Ali goes on to say, "I remember that day well. It was December 8th, 1980 when I was driving in my car with the radio playing. There was a sudden interruption of regular programming when it was announced that John Lennon was killed." Ali describes how hearing the sad news made her so emotional that she had to stop driving and pull over to regain her composure. The tragic news sent chills throughout her body as she recalled those special moments when Jilly, Mia, and herself watched and listen to The Beatles. Ali confesses that John Lennon was her favorite Beatle, but since he was married, she had to settle for Ringo instead.

Picking John Lennon's date of death as though it was her own sisters' day had worked well for her over the last twenty plus years. As Ali watched the news those first days after Lennon passed in 1980, she saw to her surprise thousands of diehard fans holding a candlelight vigil. She thought to herself, this is the day my sisters would want to be remembered. Little did Ali realize then that an amazing recurring event would take place on the anniversary of John Lennon's death. Every December 8th after sunset is memorialized by the media at the now world-famous Dakota residence of John Lennon in New York City. Ali tries to explain by associating what better day is there to remember my sisters who loved The Beatles so much than to share that day with John Lennon.

She is so upset she has a hard time breathing, and Chet reaches for her hands to show he is feeling the same pain. Tragedy always has a beginning, and the stories of Mia and Jilly are no exception. Ali exposes her emotions to Chet and describes her sister, Mia, as the type of person who always saw the better side in people and life.

Chet is overwhelmed with a feeling of being blessed to be a part of Mia and Jilly's life. He tells Ali that he desires more than ever to know everything he possibly can about Jilly and Mia. Ali tells him about her loving sister, Jilly, while they were growing up and how sad she was when she left for college. For Ali it was an emotional day in her life because it was the first time she had to say goodbye, not only to a sister, but also a best friend. Jilly always included Ali in her circle of friends, not just because of their closeness in age, but because it was the natural thing to for Jilly to do. Shortly before Jilly left for Southern Illinois University, she bought Ali her first Beatles 45 RPM record, "I Want to Hold Your Hand." Ali admitted to Chet she played it so much that her father had to constantly yell at her to stop. Ali tells Chet that she, Mia, and Jilly were avid Beatles fans.

Ali goes on to explain that Jilly told her at the age of twelve-years-old all about the facts of life. It was a time during her life that she needed to know this information, not years later when her mom got around to it. On Ali's first date when she was fourteen, Jilly gave her advice on what to do and what not to do. For each of Jilly's birthdays, their mother, Edith, would make her favorite meal: boneless fresh ham with buttered mashed potatoes, turnips, and homemade cherry pie a la mode with vanilla ice cream. Ali confesses to Chet that it was also her favorite, especially the cherry pie a la mode.

Peshtigo weather at the end of December is brutal with frigid cold winds blowing across Lake Michigan's Green Bay causing ice blocks to build up along the shore line. Ali tells Chet most late-night Christmas Eves were spent hiding under the bed covers playing with a flashlight. Jilly and Ali tried to stay awake so that they could catch a glimpse of Santa in the act of delivering his gifts. To pass time while hiding under the covers, the two would always end up telling scary stories until they both became too tired to stay awake for the arrival of Santa.

Ali recalls how mad her dad, Dave, would get when Jilly would plan her calls home around the time when her dad would not be home to avoid speaking directly with him. He was especially upset with Jilly when she told their mother that she was getting married and leaving for Vietnam. This placed Edith in an awkward position with their father, Dave, but her mother never conveyed how difficult it was to Jilly. When the family received the news that the girls were missing, Ali remembers her parents becoming deeply depressed. Edith never got over losing both Jilly and Mia and died of a broken heart only two years later. Dave had his own way of expressing his feelings which were to sit in the silence in his favorite reclining chair, shutting out the entire world, including Ali and Edith. When he lost Edith, Dave became a total recluse, never leaving the house again. Ali spoke of taking care of her father's every need until the day he died. Wiping tears from her eyes, Ali told Chet that her dad died within a year of her mom which left Ali losing the four most important people in her life in a very short period. The loss of her father didn't hit her emotionally until after his funeral when she returned home and took her first glimpse of his empty reclining chair. Losing her entire family, including Mia whom she loved as much as a sister, was devastating for Ali. It took her many years to get over her loss and to move on with her life.

Ali asks, "I always wondered why their husbands, Ricky and George, never got in touch with the family in Peshtigo?"

Chet painfully tells Ali, "I wish I had a better explanation, but Ricky and George were killed about three weeks after Mia and Jilly went missing."

Ali responds, "Oh, my God, I can't believe it." Ali apologizes for her parents ignoring George and Ricky during and after the disappearances and admits they were so engrossed, they never gave them a thought. Especially when Ali describes how George and Ricky's relationship with Edith was always on good terms.

The bartender returns to take their orders, but Ali is now not hungry and only orders a small California salad. Chet orders an iron steak which is served in a sizzling hot skillet with creamed spinach. Chet signals the bartender for another Jack Daniels while Ali passes on her third Cosmo.

The sense of comfort while speaking with Chet leads Ali to open her heart, and she continues to describe her memories of Mia. She loved Mia from the very first moment they met. She remembers Mia appearing very nervous. At the time, Jilly had already told her about the sad fate of Mia's parents being killed in an auto accident. The first time Mia walked into the Landry home, she brought two gift wrapped presents which she hid behind her back. Mia handed the larger gift to Edith and the smaller one to Ali. Not wasting a moment of time, Ali tore open her gift to reveal a new Milton Brady game called "Flip Your Wig" which was about the Beatles. Ali was stunned and could only utter the words, "Oh, my God, it's the Beatles." Edith opened her gift which was a shrink-wrapped basket filled with jars of nuts, cheese, and cooking spices. Both Edith and Ali gave Mia a big thank you and a loving hug. Ali began telling Chet detailed stories about how much she enjoyed the "Flip Your Wig" game and how it was played endless times by the girls including Edith. Ali mentions the fact that the silly game is still in her possession and that she occasionally opens the box envisioning Edith, Jilly, and Mia sitting at the kitchen table, laughing along with her as their favorite Beatle playing piece moved around the board game.

Through Ali's eyes, Mia was a clone of Jilly, and it was her feeling that they were cut from the same mold. Ali felt that Jilly and Mia were inseparable and loved each other very much. Ali told Chet that Edith treated Mia as her third daughter. When speaking with family and friends, Edith always told everyone she had three daughters. Chet responds, "That explains why you refer to Mia a sister."

A remarkable thought suddenly comes into Ali's mind, and she tells the story of when Mia was eleven-years-old. It was a stinging, cold winter day when Mia's parents dropped her off at her Grammy's house and promised they would be gone only overnight. They were going to make the long drive to attend a family funeral in Danville, IL. Mia confided in Ali telling her that she had frequent nightmares about waving goodbye to her mom and dad as they drove away in their 1947 Oldsmobile woody wagon. In that recurring dream, her mom was waving back. She was wearing white gloves as she waved and smiled, gazing into Mia's eyes. Mia never forgot her parents dying in that fierce snow storm attempting to keep their promise to return to Quincy and pick her up from her Grammy's. Losing her parents haunted Mia her whole life, and she always thought it was because of her that they died. Ali placed Mia on a pedestal, using the words loving, caring, enthusiastic, and thoughtful when describing the young woman, she called her new-found sister.

Chet promises Ali that he will do everything in his power to correct the legacy of Jilly and Mia and have them both honored for their valor. Ali thanks him for what he is doing to rectify a terrible wrong. She tells him that she feels the presence of Mia and Jilly watching over Chet. She relays to him that she feels they are at peace knowing that there is someone who truly cares about finding out the truth.

Ali and Chet reach the point where they are comfortable talking about themselves and the unhappy stories of losing their spouses to cancer. Ali is a special events coordinator for Carver Yachts based in Pulaski, WI and travels around the country to various tradeshow events. Carver Boat Corp. started in 1954 building small molded veneer wooden runabout boats. The company set up its first factory in Milwaukee, but moved it to Pulaski near Green Bay by 1957. The name of the company was taken from the first three letters of the two founders last names, Carter and Verhaegen. In 1963 the company began to gradually offer larger boats. In the late 1960's, the company made the move from wood to fiberglass construction. Carver was one of the last hold outs in the wooden boat field, resisting the change to fiberglass. In 1982 they introduced a new "aft cabin" style boat that would soon define Carver as a motor yacht builder.

Chet tells Ali that he has recently retired having had a thirty-five-year career with the mid-sized insurance broker company, Boyce Insurance Agency. Their life experience stories are just too similar for any common occurrence, and they both look at each other with mutual respect.

Ali finally decides to have her third Cosmo. When it arrives, she proposes a toast to Chet saying, "Here is to the both of us."

Chet adds, "Staying good friends forever," as their glasses meet with a clink. This is a moment between Ali and Chet where they begin to appreciate each other as more than just friends. They are both discovering that together they may be able to fill the voids within each other's lives.

The jazz trio stopped playing over two hours ago, and the bartender announces the last call. Chet can't believe that time has passed so quickly. Ali also agrees. She tells Chet that she has a meeting at 8:00 am. Sipping the residue of what was left in her glass, Ali calls it a night. Chet offers to walk her to her room. He finally reaches into his jacket pocket, pulling out the two dog tags and one wedding band, and hands them to Ali. Ali, with an astonished look on her face, quickly reads the names and instantly realizes what is in the palm of her hand. Examining the ring, she reads the inscription and asks this is Jilly's wedding band, where is Mia's? "I don't know," replies Chet, but in his mind he feels strongly about the accuracy of his daydream when Mia told him she swallowed her ring. Should he tell her? Will telling her make her think he is crazy? The moment arrives where Ali finally loses control of her emotions, and she quietly cries softly like a baby. Chet gives in and decides to take his chances and opens his heart, telling Ali about his dream. Ali's crying stops, and she closely listens to Chet as he describes having a conversation with her sisters in his car on a recent trip to Washington.

Chet confesses that it was hearing the gurgling sounds which pulled him back to Vietnam. In his mind, it was too much of a coincidence that the gurgling sounds stopped when Ta led him to the spot where Mia and Jilly died. He firmly believes his dream of Mia and Jilly sitting in his car, telling him the story of why there was only one wedding band found is exactly what happened. Ali is a realistic thinker and doesn't agree with Chet's belief, but doesn't want to upset him. Clutching the dog tags and wedding band, she raises her hand and tells Chet, "These are the only personal items I have left of my sisters. After my mother passed away, my father was still so angry at Jilly for not trusting him that he threw away all her personal belongings."

With tears still streaming down her face, Ali presses eight floor button in the elevator. Chet remarks that he also is on the same floor. The elevator bell rings, the door opens. While walking down the hall to Ali's room, Chet wonders if this will be their final goodbye. When they reach Ali's room, she suddenly stops and asks Chet to make sure this isn't the last time they see each other. Chet being very happy to hear Ali say those words leans toward her. Ali closes her eyes as they embrace and gently kiss. Deep in Chet's mind there is a rebirth of his soul, offering him a new beginning to emotionally absorb.

Chapter 10

2005 Kiawah Island, SC

Back in Kiawah Island, Chet's telephone is endlessly ringing. Chet purposely avoids answering his home phone because most of the time the callers are solicitors. Chet reluctantly answers and is greeted by Dr. Carter who is checking in to see if there has been any change of heart regarding his chemo and radiation treatment. Knowing now that there will be a light burning brighter somewhere in his future, Chet acknowledges that he must start to address his health issues. Dr. Carter goes into a lengthy speech telling Chet that he must consider his health treatment options and decide the best course of action as soon as possible. The doctor explains that time is running out if he wants to try to extend his life. Dr. Carter tells Chet about a new treatment called Proton Therapy and mentions that the new treatment is only available at five different cancer treatment centers spread out throughout the United States. Dr. Carter explains further that Proton Therapy is an advanced form of radiation therapy that destroys cancer cells by preventing them from dividing and growing the same as with standard X-ray radiation. Proton Therapy uses protons positively charged atomic particles instead of the protons used in standard X-ray radiation therapy. Dr. Carter goes on to say that with proton therapy, doctors can precisely target the tumor while minimizing damage to the surrounding healthy tissue. Unlike X-ray radiation, such as intensity-modulated radiation therapy, protons deposit much of their radiation directly in the tumor and then stop. Chet realizes that this is a lot of information to absorb all at once. His mechanical knowledge in manufacturing helps him to understand the basic mechanics of the treatment, but he still needs to sort out the rest so that he fully understands what Dr. Carter is trying to convey.

The closest hospital offering Proton therapy is Emory Medical Center in Atlanta. Chet is given the news that treatment must be approved on a patient by patient basis by a special board of radiologists. The doctor explains since so many patients desire treatment, it must be rationed, and only the few who meet the rigid criteria are accepted. Dr. Carter convinces Chet that he has nothing to lose if he applied and since he's a Vietnam Veteran who handled "Agent Orange," it might give him an edge. He must first come in for a thorough examination followed by CAT/CT and maybe a PET scan. Dr. Carter describes in detail about computed tomography, more commonly known as a CT or CAT scan. It is a diagnostic medical test which, like traditional X-rays, produces multiple images or pictures of the inside of the body. Dr. Carter asks, "Did I lose you yet?"

Chet responds, "No, I think I'm okay so far."

Very slowly Dr. Carter describes the cross-sectional images generated during a CT scan can be reformatted in multiple planes, even generating three-dimensional images. These images can be viewed on a computer monitor, printed on film, or transferred to a CD or DVD. CT images of internal organs, bones, soft tissue, and blood vessels typically provide greater detail than traditional X-rays, particularly of soft tissues and blood vessels.

Dr. Carter further explains that PET is short for Positron Emission Tomography. A PET can show how body tissues are working, as well as what they look like. The doctor goes into the cost explaining that PET scanners are very expensive, and only a few hospitals have them. Roper St. Francis is fortunate enough to have these special machines which means Chet will not have to travel a long distance for treatment. Dr. Carter advises that not everyone who has cancer will need to have a PET scan, but as far as he can tell, Chet is a good candidate. Chet slowly nods his head and tells the doctor he understands the treatment.

It was clarified again by Dr. Carter that the two types of scans will be performed at nearby Roper St. Francis Hospital in Charleston. Once the exam and scans are analyzed by a team of radiologists, the results will be sent to Emory where it could take up to two weeks before a decision is rendered. An appointment is confirmed by Chet with Dr. Carter for this upcoming Monday. Doctor Carter also tells Chet that if he is turned down for Proton Therapy, there is a second option which is a partial liver transplant. The doctor suggests that one of his children may be a donor candidate and explains that donating a partial liver will not affect them living a normal life. Chet is advised by Dr. Carter that if his children are willing, they should give blood specimens at their own local testing labs as soon as possible so all will be ready if he is turned down at Emory Medical Center. If his children agree, Dr. Carter will email special prescriptions to Chet's children, Chester and Cathy.

Throughout his life, Chet has never felt sorry for himself. It has been a long three days since he and Ali said their goodbyes. Chet ponders how he is going to let his family and especially Ali know about his illness. He decides to call his children, beginning with his son Chester, and then his daughter Cathy. His children are both taken by surprise when hearing of their father's illness. They always thought of their father as invincible, a man who never complained, and are devastated by the news. Cathy's first thought is to rush to Kiawah and be her father's caretaker. Chet nonchalantly waves off the offer. Chet explains that the last thing he wants is to shake up the lives of the people he loves. His health treatment options are clearly explained to Chester and Cathy, giving them at least something to hope for. Chester and Cathy immediately offer to be potential donors and agree to have blood tests taken. Chet tells his children that he hopes the second option doesn't take place, but if it does, he will be ready to quickly place the wheels in motion. Before saying his good byes, Chet announces that he has recently met a special person on a recent trip to Chicago, and her name is Ali Parker. His daughter Cathy wants to know more about her dad's new friend, but is overcome with the bad news of his health and decides to continue the conversation at another time.

Sitting by the large window in his living room which faces the beach and open Atlantic Ocean, Chet realizes he has a question that needs to be answered. Should this be the time to tell Ali about his illness? Looking beyond the horizon, he focuses on the cumulus clouds slowly floating by. They remind him of Nancy and feels as though she is trying to tell him that it was okay.

Chet reaches for his phone to call Ali. The time of day makes Chet wonder if she is home from work yet, but he still dials her number anyway. Ali picks up on the second ring knowing by her caller ID that it is Chet. Hearing Chet's voice gives her goose bumps. She immediately admits to him that he has been on her mind ever since their goodbye in Chicago. Hearing those words, Chet realizes that their feelings for each other are mutual. Paying very close attention to Chet's every word, Ali senses something is on his mind. Realizing that he is spinning his words, Chet bluntly tells Ali there is something he must tell her.

Searching his soul, Chet carefully details his health condition hoping that it will not frighten her away. Very calmly Chet describes his handling of "Agent Orange" during the Vietnam War, spraying the defoliant along river banks. He admits that his Navy training didn't cover the handling or give instructions for "Agent Orange." This caused him and his shipmates, on frequent occasions, to absorb and inhale the mist during spray-back applications. Ali listens very closely to Chet's words. Hearing the words "Agent Orange" runs electrified shocks up and down her spine, and she wonders what the outcome will be. Ali's first instinct is to think the worst, but her feelings toward Chet urge her to be there for him to help him in any way she can.

In his own weird way, Chet was thinking that the last thing Ali needed was another cancer victim in her life. After an eternally long pause, Ali replies that she doesn't want him to feel that he would be a burden to her and wants to be there for him. She tells him that she has some vacation time due and will travel to Kiawah Island next week after his tests have been completed. Chet realizes Ali is willing to stand by his side, knowing how difficult the journey may be. Having someone to love will help Chet override the physical and mental pain of his impending journey.

From Chet's window, he watches the sun slowly rise over the Atlantic, creating a view too beautiful to miss. Chet intensely watches the gradual blending of crimson and yellow skies. The agonizing wait to begin his tests finally comes to an end. Severe abdominal pains cause a sleepless night for Chet. He welcomes the new day with a passion to live. Catching the warm rays of a new day's morning sun, Chet takes his first steps out of bed. His bedroom begins to spin and the view of the sun's rays become wavy. Chet falls back onto the bed. Glancing at the dresser, his clock reads 7:05. He has never experienced this feeling before. He feels as though he is drunk, closing his eyes help to cut off the spinning bedroom. Chet doesn't want to call for help and decides to just lay in bed and wait, hoping to recover from his dizziness.

An hour has passed since his last try to stand up, and the room has stopped spinning, but he is still slightly dizzy. Chet forces himself to get out of bed, holding on to what he can, he makes his way to the bathroom. He slowly walks into the shower, holding on to the shower door for dear life. Still in his underwear, Chet turns on the cold water, shivering he hopes the cold will help pass the dizziness. After ten minutes of cold water running over his body, Chet begins to feel the dizziness subside. He knows that he will be late for his appointment, but plans on not mentioning his dizziness to Dr. Carter.

Roper St. Francis Hospital is a forty-five minute drive from Chet's home; it is already 8:45, and his appointment is at 9:00. Realizing that racing to get to the hospital will not do him any good, Chet comes up with the excuse to give Dr. Carter for blaming his lateness on a flat tire. By the time Chet arrives at Roper Hospital, his dizziness is completely gone. He rushes up the stairs to the radiology department and runs into Dr. Carter. Looking down his glasses, the doctor says to Chet, "I thought you changed your mind!"

Smiling back, Chet says, "I'm ready to rumble!"

Chet is told to change into a hospital gown and lay down on a bed. His vital signs are taken by a nurse who takes blood samples and finally injects him with a mild sedative to slow down his rapid heartbeat. Chet begins to take deep breathes and slowly falls into a semi-sleep. Overhead lights glaring in his face, Chet is awakened by Dr. Carter who asks if he has been having dizzy spells. Chet, who never was a liar, confesses that he had one earlier that morning when he tried to step out of bed. Dr. Carter expresses to Chet that his platelet count is severely low, and it's a miracle he could drive to the hospital. The doctor wants to keep Chet hospitalized for further testing and an immediate intravenous infusion of platelets. Chet hurriedly attempts to sit up in the bed and realizes he can't even raise his head off the pillow. Dr. Carter hands Chet his cellphone and makes the comment, "Call whomever you need to call now! The final test results won't be in for another day or two."

Hospitals were never a place Chet liked to visit, and the nursing staff got a real taste of Chet's unwillingness to be a patient. Not acting himself, Chet wants no part of being held hostage and demands the nursing staff to let him go home. With his comments to Dr. Carter falling on deaf ears, Dr. Carter tells Chet to stop acting like a baby, look around at your fellow patients, and you will see real suffering. Chet stops complaining and begins to ponder his recent trip to Vietnam and his meeting with Ta. He begins to compare the horrendous treatment Mia and Jilly endured to his current situation. With teary eyes, Chet decides to call his children to inform them of his stay at Roper. Chet struggles trying to find the right words. He wonders how his children will accept his new health condition. Will they afford him the same love as he is accustomed to, or will they just give him pity?

He calls his daughter, Cathy first, thinking that she will not be angry at him for holding back his symptoms to her and Dr. Carter. Chet tries to explain that being ill is all new to him and is something that he needs to get used to. Cathy once again offers to take the trip to Kiawah, but Chet convinces her that it is not necessary and promises to let her know if things change. Cathy says, "I'm going to call you every day while you're in the hospital and if I sense something is wrong, I'm coming down to Kiawah as soon as possible."

Calling his son, Chester, is much different than speaking to his daughter, and Chet expects to be crossed examined as though he was on a witness stand during a murder trial. But Chester pleasantly surprises Chet when they speak, and their conversation goes well, and his son is very understanding. Chester wants his father to know that he will do anything to help him. Chet again down plays any need for Chester to rush to Kiawah and promises to speak to him on the phone each day he is in the hospital. Their conversation ends with Chester telling his father, "I love you, Dad."

Chet deeply inhales, holds his breath, and as he slowly exhales, feels the pain subside. Chet calls Ali and as soon as she speaks, he feels more at ease. Her soothing voice provides Chet with a feeling of happiness. He realizes Ali is the catalyst who now allows him the ability to focus on beating his cancer. With only the sound of her voice, Ali seems to tame Chet's bad mood. Chet recognizes that Ali's ability to smooth out his moodiness is a special component of love. He is now more than ever willing to make Ali part of his life.

On his third day at Roper, right after breakfast, staring out the window and trying to watch reruns of the "Golden Girls," Chet hears a knock at the door. Chet turns his head and suddenly sees Ali standing at the door looking even more beautiful than he remembered. She walks over to the bed and gives him a kiss on his lips and strokes his face with both her hands. Just being able to see and touch Ali's hand turns his bad patient behavior into the better man he is. Chet tells Ali that he spoke to his children last night and it made him feel so good to speak with them. He tells Ali that his son, Chester, and daughter, Cathy, wanted to rush down to see him, but he didn't think it was necessary. Seeing Ali now in person reaffirms he made the right decision.

Dr. Carter strolls into the room with a bunch of papers clutched in his hand, and Chet introduces the doctor to Ali. Dr. Carter then asks to speak to Chet in private, but Chet tells the doctor it's okay to talk with Ali in the room. Bracing himself for bad news, Chet reaches out for Ali's hand to hold as though they are now combined in a single spirit. Dr. Carter begins his overview of the CAT/CT and PET scans by saying, "I have some bad news." The bottom line in Dr. Carter's findings is that the growth on Chet's liver has slightly increased in size. Dr. Carter surmises that the growth may be cancerous due to the rate of growth. Dr. Carter also informs Chet that he has called Emory Medical Center in Atlanta and requested them to speed up their decision for Proton Therapy.

What seems like minor good news, Dr. Carter reveals that Chet's platelet count is back to near normal levels thanks to the infusions he received. Dr. Carter relays that he will sign the paperwork to have Chet released so he can go home and rest. The decision to start regular chemo and radiation treatment will be delayed a couple of days giving Emory Medical some time to respond to Dr. Carter's rush request. Dr. Carter doesn't want to begin a regular radiation regimen that must be stopped when Proton Therapy begins. When Dr. Carter leaves the room, Chet requests Ali to find the head nurse and have her come to his room. When Ali and the head nurse return to his room, Chet apologizes to the nurse. He asks that she spread his message to the entire nursing staff. The nurse shakes Chet's hand and says, "This will make my staff very happy. Thank you, Mr. Ross." When the head nurse leaves the room, Ali gives Chet a strange look and Chet responds by saying, "I acted like a fool, and I'm now very sorry." Ali accepts the explanation and asks Chet, "Are you afraid of what lies ahead because if you are, I'm here for you."

Being afraid of death is nothing new to Chet who explains to Ali that he has come close with death twice in his life. Ali says, "Please, tell me, I need to know everything about you." Chet never enjoyed talking about his war years, especially the close calls with death. Only his wife Nancy and two children are aware of his private war stories. Ali sits and patiently waits for an answer. Chet finally decides to let her into his dark world of his near-death experiences. Chet begins with his story of receiving a bullet wound as a crew member of

PCF-33 and almost bleeding to death. He tells Ali that if it were not for the quick thinking of his crew to rush him back to base and the nurses and doctors on the hospital ship "Heilen," he would have bled to death. Chet admits that he was mostly unconscious during the entire event, and his memory is vague. But according to his shipmates, he was told they never would give up on him while constantly trying to stop the bleeding. Ali squeezes Chet's hand as though she was feeling the same pain.

Chet asks, "Do you want me to continue? Are you okay?"

Ali replies, "Yes, Chet, I'm okay. Please continue." Chet begins to tell Ali of his second brush with death. He mentions that PCF-33 had a chocolate lab named Buck who served as a war dog. Buck and his trainer, Rugby, gave the swift boat a special set of advantages over other swift boats. PCF-33 had the extra tools of intense sight, smell, and hearing. Chet clearly recalls the day as if it were yesterday. It was a dry, hot, and humid day when PCF-33 was ambushed by the Viet Cong on both sides of the Perfume River which is a very dangerous situation that most swift boats commanders learn to avoid. Lt. Commander Horner decided to retreat, change course rapidly, and turn around. Unknown to the crew while we were firefighting up river, the Viet Cong had floated tree logs down river. Once we were turned around, Horner gave the command, "All ahead full," and PCF-33 came up on plane very quickly and within a thirty second period, we were travelling at 40 knots. By this time the floating logs were a quarter mile straight ahead barely visible and almost impossible to see when travelling at that speed. I was standing at the gunner's nest when, without any warning, Horner saw the floating logs ahead and knew if the swift boat hit one at that speed, we would have capsized. Horner gave the order for a hard right rutter, and the boat sharply turned which caused me to lose my balance and fall out of the gunner's nest, hitting my head on the deck and bouncing into the water. I was dazed and trying to keep afloat. I remember hearing Buck barking from the boat and seeing him jump into the river towards me. Buck kept on barking and swimming towards me as though he knew I was in danger. Rugby grabbed the megaphone and yelled out to me, "Alligator at three o'clock." I turned my head and saw a giant alligator rapidly approaching. The next thing I knew, Buck was at my side barking and trying to get the alligator's attention. Buck then swam toward the alligator and used himself as a decoy for diversion. It worked and the alligator began to chase Buck who lead it away from me. Finally, PCF-33 came along side me and lifted me out of the water. When I finally stood on deck, I saw Buck still trying to swim away from the alligator. I climbed back into the gunner's nest and took aim at the alligator who by now was only about ten feet behind Buck. Pressing the trigger, I sent a spray of bullets that cut up that alligator into pieces. Ali is memorized by the story and asks Chet, "Whatever happened to Buck?"

Chet replies, "We fished him out of the water, and I gave him a big hug as he frantically licked my face."

On a sad note, Chet tries to delicately explain to Ali that he loved Buck very much, and he was a vital part of his life in 1968. Chet admits that he will never forget Buck and what he did to save his life. Chet explains that trainer Rugby left the Navy in 1970, and he wanted to take Buck back home to Trenton, NJ, but the chain of command wouldn't allow it. Buck was then reassigned to a new trainer who kept in touch with Rugby and always filled Chet in with a Christmas card every year until 1973. Ali asks, "What happened in 1973?"

Chet responds, "The war was winding down, and U.S. forces were beginning to withdraw. It was decided that all war dogs were treated as government surplus; some were given to the South Vietnamese government and others were euthanized."

Ali inquisitively asks, "Where did Buck end up?"

Chet, trying to hold back his feelings, sadly says, "Buck was euthanized."

Ali says, "How cruel can we be? That dog was a hero, not government surplus."

Chet is finally home. As they are walking towards his front door, Ali sees for the first time the Atlantic Ocean with a crimson sky reflecting over the water. This is a completely unfamiliar sight to Ali. Her eyes try to absorb nature's beauty and the peaceful spell it places on her soul. Ali has agreed to stay at Chet's Kiawah Island home so that she can be of help should his health diminish. Staying together under the same roof makes sense to her and Chet. Appearances do lie, and anyone not aware of Chet's ailment would never know by looking at him.

Walking into Chet's home, Ali becomes mesmerized from the higher elevation view of the ocean. Looking through the panoramic windows becomes Ali's new obsession. Chet wraps his arms around her from behind. As she turns to face him, they hug and hold a kiss. Chet shows Ali the quest room where Chet drops her two small bags and tells her to meet him in the den in twenty minutes. His plans are to go out for dinner at a local low country style restaurant called Riptide where the best low country style cooking can be found.

When they arrive at the Riptide restaurant, Ali is not familiar with low country cooking and asks Chet to order for her. When the waiter arrives, Chet orders for two starting with cooter soup, shrimp and grits, and a side of fried cabbage. Ali asks, "What is cooter soup?" and Chet replies, "It's a local favorite! You'll love it." While waiting for their food to arrive, they begin to catch up on what each of them has been doing since they last saw each other. Ali gazes at Chet and as she looks into his eyes, Chet tells her how happy he is that she is with him. The romantic atmosphere at the Riptide is a perfect place for catching up on events in their lives without ever having to mention Chet's health status.

When they arrive back home, Chet walks to the built-in bar and pours two glasses of Chardonnay. He asks Ali to follow him to the outdoor deck. With a slight chill in the air that doesn't seem to bother them, Chet pulls two lounge chairs together. Nothing but a harvest moon between them, Ali makes a toast to their future, and they once again hold a long kiss. Chet tells Ali how much he enjoys looking out over the ocean, soaking in the beauty. He compares the beauty of Ali to the ocean view and tells her he is in love. Even though they have only recently met, Ali feels a special reconnection to her sisters because of Chet. She responds to Chet in a low tone voice, "I love you too."

After the last sip of wine, Chet reaches out for Ali's hand leading her to his bedroom. They both passionately kiss and embrace. Falling on the king size bed, they start to undress each other, and they travel to the point of no return. The love making tenderly flows, and both Chet and Ali reach their long-lost desires. As the full moon shines brightly across the still Atlantic Ocean, two people who have become good friends now become tender lovers. The intimacy of sharing the same bed with Ali diminishes Chet's fears of his looming well-being.

Each dawn and dusk, the new-found couple make it a point to walk the seafoam lined beach of Kiawah Island. The couple leisurely strolls by many shells and sand dollars as well as the occasional starfish. Ali always stops when she sees a starfish and tosses them back, hoping that they have more life to live. Arm and arm, Ali and Chet live each day as it comes without thinking of any health issues. Feeding seagulls in the morning mist becomes one of Ali's passions as Chet witnesses it in a childlike type gratification. Even a simple thing such as watching Ali walk on the beach in the South Carolina rain gives him goose bumps. He knows that his love for Nancy will never dwindle, yet Chet now feels the same reawakening of that love for Ali.

After returning from a walk one morning, Chet notices a blinking red light on his answering machine. He and Ali move toward the red light, and Chet presses the play button. The call was from Ken Gallagher of the DOD informing him that after reviewing the case files, the DOD will classify Mia Flynn and Jill Landry as MIA "Killed in captivity." The moment those words are heard, Ali bursts into tears, and Chet gets glassy eyed. Ali falls into Chet's arms, crying, "You did it! You did it!" Chet is pleasantly surprised by the decision. He realizes that waiting patiently for the federal govern-ments review and response was not easy, but absolutely worth the wait. Gallagher goes on to say in his message that both girls will now officially be honored. Their names will be added to the names at the Vietnam Women's Memorial on the grounds of the Vietnam Veteran's Memorial in Washing-ton, D.C. The Vietnam Women's Memorial will soon be in contact with him to discuss the way the girls will be honored and their names added to the memorial.

Satisfaction isn't a new word in Chet's vocabulary; his lifetime of results in the workplace have always set the pace for accomplishments. Ali breaks into a cold sweat, walks out to the deck to get some fresh air, and stares up toward the sky. Chet follows and leans over towards her. While holding both her hands, he says to her, "This is a good day."

Ali responds, "I know both Jilly and Mia are now looking down upon us with grateful hearts."

Over the next three days, watching ocean tides come and go, Ali and Chet continue to share the beauty and advantages of oceanfront living. Time itself seems to be placed on hold for the couple. Ali and Chet take in all that they can and relish each other's presence, sharing laughter, camaraderie, and love making.

A phone ringing at 7:00 am is not a good sign, and this day is no exception. Chet's complexion turns gray as he answers a phone call from Dr. Carter. The doctor is asked to hold on while Ali grabs another extension so she can listen in on the conversation. Ali and Chet listen to Dr. Carter as he tells them the bad news of Chet not being accepted into Proton Therapy. Emory Medical Center's head radiologist explained that the demand is too large with over eight hundred cancer patients on their waiting list. Their criterion was based on Chet's age and the advanced state of his cancer along with its location in his liver. Chet remains completely silent and stunned. All that is heard is the soft whimpering of Ali who is listening in on the other line.

Chet is in no mood to hear Dr. Carter's plan to begin the second option of partial liver transplant as soon as possible. The doctor informs Chet that he has gone over his children's blood tests and finds that his son is a perfect match. Chet tells the doctor he must ponder his options and hangs up. Ali comes running from the other room and jumps into Chet's arms, and they embrace. Reaching a fork in the road of his life, Chet realizes to live he must now ask his son to donate part of his liver to save his life. Chet would gladly give his life for any of his children or grandchildren, but to view it in reverse is very hard for him to grasp. Ali willingly gives her approval to whatever Chet decides and tells him she will stand by his side no matter what. Chet says to her, "This isn't a good day."

Understanding that Chet needed space to think, Ali retreats to a private place in the house to allow him to take his time in making a very difficult decision. Chet grabs a sweater and rests in a lounge chair on the outdoor deck. Taking in his favorite view listening to the sounds of the surf breaking on the shore, Chet wanders off in deep thought. Chet silently asks his beloved wife, Nancy, for her guidance in coming to the right decision. Chet recalls a moment in his past when he and Nancy had a conversation concerning her chemo and radiation treatment. Thinking that this would produce the best results, Chet had persuaded Nancy to seek treatment against her will. Her reasoning was that she didn't want to slowly wilt away while attempting to prevent the unpreventable. Chet now understands what Nancy meant by those words and sadly realizes that he selfishly pushed his beliefs on her. In not listening to Nancy's wishes, Chet feels responsible for her suffering. He doesn't want to die or leave Ali, but he accepts Doctor Carter's option to have a partial liver transplant. Chet ultimately concludes that the time he has left should be as painless as possible for himself as well as for his loved ones. After spiritually witnessing his own wilting away from the effects of regular chemo and radiation treatments before an audience of loved ones, he makes the decision to call his son, Chester.

After a few hours, Ali comes to check on Chet and finds him standing on the deck. As she opens the sliding door, Chet turns and immediately makes eye contact with her. He smiles slightly, and Ali realizes without a word being spoken that Chet has reached a decision. While clutching each other's hand tightly, Ali tells Chet she understands why he decided to seek a partial liver transplant. Chet affirms by saying, "I want to spend what's left of my life with you and my family, so let's make the best of the time we have left."

Ali responds, "I love you, Chet."

Ali decides to share two stories with Chet about her sisters. The first story is about when Mia was in her second week at Southern Illinois University. She had to return to Quincy to settle some of her Grammy's estate matters. Torrential rains made driving almost impossible with limited visibility. Slightly north of St. Louis, Mia came upon a vehicle with its driver's door wide open. The car had spun out and hit the median which divided the north and southbound traffic. Not paying attention to the danger of stopping on the highway and with zero visibility, she pulled over in front of the other car. There was a strong rushing flow of water by the median making the attempt to walk through it very difficult. There was no sign of the driver, and the engine was still running. After searching the surrounding area, Mia observed something red lying in the water. As Mia raced to get a better look at what the object was, she realized that it was a body lying face down in the rushing water. She immediately flipped the person over, sees that it is a man, and drags him to higher ground. As Mia begins to resuscitate the man, he slowly begins to gasp for air. She sees a large gash in his left leg. Seeing that the leg is bleeding profusely, Mia rushes back to her car and grabs a tire iron and a towel in her trunk. The man is still unconscious but breathing as Mia rips and wraps the towel around his leg and uses the tire iron to tighten the hold. Mia's quick response and decision to use a tourniquet works. The bleeding stops, and the man's life was saved. Although the bleeding had subsided, Mia knew that she must keep him as dry and warm as possible to prevent him from going into shock. The man she saved was married and a father of three children.

Ali explains that the man's name was Bill Archer who lived in Pekin, IL when he was in the process of driving home after a business trip. Bill Archer and his wife, Debbie, called Mia on each of the anniversaries of Bill's accident and always had their two young children thank Mia for saving their dad. Mia looked forward to the call each year displaying a special spark of appreciation and gratification. During the following Christmas, Mia received photo Christmas cards each year showing the whole family in a holiday pose. After Mia and Jilly went missing, Bill Archer and his wife, Debbie, didn't receive a response to their annual phone call, but however they could, find and located my parents phone number. Ali's voice breaks as she tries to explain how devastated the Archers' were when they found out Mia and Jilly were missing. Bill Archer called every week for over a year asking if we heard any news about the girls' disappearances. Ali says, "I think Bill Archer and his wife felt so helpless and distressed, they took the loss as though it was their own family."

Ali's second story involved Jilly when she was in high school. A widow neighbor in her seventies had come down with cancer. It was during the summer of 1964, and Jilly volunteered to be her caretaker until the woman's family could come up with the funds to hire a fulltime caretaker. Jilly cared for the neighbor most of the summer, giving up spending time with her friends. Ali tells Chet that taking care of her sick neighbor helped her sister to make up her mind about becoming a nurse. Jilly realized caring for people who are in need overshadowed her own social life. Ali looks at Chet and tells him, "I will give you that same care and dedication my sisters gave to others."

It was cold and foggy when Chet and Ali awoke the next morning. Chet had a difficult night with extremely strong abdominal pains. After a light breakfast, Chet decides to take the short walk to his mailbox. He is surprised to find a letter from the Vietnam Women's Memorial in Washington, D.C. Slowly opening the envelope, Chet begins to read and is thrilled to find out that the memorial wants to have a special event honoring those women civilians who gave their lives during the Vietnam War. The ceremony will be held on Veteran's Day and will have as its honorees Mia Flynn and Jill Landry. The memorial will be distributing a press release describing in detail the unique stories of both women. They are expecting several thousand people to attend. Overwhelmed with the news, Chet walks towards the house as quickly as his pain will allow. He is so excited to read the letter to Ali. Chet calls for Ali to come into the living room. They sit close together on the sofa, and Chet reads the letter he has received from the Vietnam Women's Memorial. Ali is so overwhelmed to hear the news, she bows her head and begins to cry. Chet caresses Ali and says, "The cries of Mia and Jilly will now finally be heard."

Chapter 11

2006 Kiawah Island, SC

Another early morning call from Dr. Carter reveals that the transplant is scheduled to take place at Roper Hospital in three days. The periods of pain Chet has been experiencing have increased and he begins to develop other symptoms. Chet finds it more and more difficult to live a normal life. Weakness and dizziness are the new order of the day. His skin now has a yellowish tint noticeable not only to Chet, but to his family. At the suggestion of Ali, a wheel chair is purchased so Chet can have more mobility. Most days Chet finds himself sitting in his wheel chair holding the dog tags and wedding band, replaying his version of some of the stories told to him by Ta. Chet repeatedly relives a moment in the girls' last days before Typhoon Cobra when they were brutalized by the Viet Cong. According to conversations Chet had with Ta, special torture treatments were devised when the girls refused to perform their requested heinous acts.

Ta explained to Chet that the Viet Cong huts were situated near a very large nest of a notorious creature called the black biting ant. Similar to fire ants, these predators are black, larger in size, and have their nests above ground. They are extremely poisonous, and one ant can kill with just a few bites. These nests are usually made up of thousands of ants. Ta gave a bleak description of black biting ants and their extreme aggressiveness telling Chet that a nest will eat the flesh of a human in a short period of time.

The girls were tied to stakes and carried over to the black biting ant nest. The Viet Cong would take a dead rat and put it on a stick and feed the ants while the girls watched. It took only a few minutes for the ants to devour the rat. Then the girls' faces were placed within an inch of the nest while they screamed and cried out loud. Ta only recalls watching this form of torture twice as the girls always submitted themselves after just the threat of the ants. Reaching into his memory, Ta also explained another torture which the Viet Cong used on Mia and Jilly. They were hung naked at night upside down by their ankles over the river waterline. Their bodies were placed in such a position that if they relaxed or fell asleep their nose and mouths would fall below the waterline. As Ta conveyed to Chet, the Viet Cong watched and enjoyed this torture treatment just out of pure sadistic pleasure.

Instead of thinking about his own medical condition, Chet focuses on the fact that his pain in no way compares to the torture and pain that Mia and Jilly endured. Holding and rubbing the dog tags and wedding band, Chet prays for Mia and Jilly as the starry, starry night hypnotizes him to sleep.

Ali suggests and works out arrangements with Chet's family to come and visit to spend as much time as possible together prior to Chet's operation. The importance of spending time with his family is something Ali wants for Chet, even though at times he doesn't want visitors. Chester and Cathy are extremely thankful to Ali for her caregiving to their father. Both agree that having someone for him to love will help him accept his decision regarding the transplant and the recovery days ahead.

Dr. Carter once again calls to inform Chet that the operation will take place on November 11th at 9 am. Even though it's a holiday, special arrangements have been made by the hospital and the surgeon. Dr. Carter explains that a surgeon friend of his named Dr. Graham will be performing the surgery. Dr. Graham is considered one of the best surgeons in the region specializing in liver transplants. Dr. Graham is only available to drive into Kiawah Island on November 11th. As soon as Chet ends his call with Dr. Carter, the phone rings again, this time it is his son, Chester. Chet and Chester tell each other how much they love each other while both breaking down in tears. Chester wants his father to know that he is so proud him of him and relays that if the tables were turned, Chet will answer the call of duty just like he did in Vietnam. Chet is extremely moved when he hears Chester's words and says, "Son, your mother would be so proud of you. I'm sure she'll be looking over the both us during the procedure."

As November 11th approaches, both Ali and Chet understand that he and Chester will be unable to attend the Vietnam Women's Memorial ceremony. Chet begins to receive many phone messages from CNN, FOX News, and other media organizations all wanting to interview Chet before the event so they can air a special report. Ali doesn't want to leave Chet home while she attends the ceremony. Chet conveys with all the strength he has that her attendance is now vital to his wishes. Chet tells Ali that giving her sisters' stories to the world is the most important thing she can do. Ali reluctantly agrees. She comes to the realization that Jilly and Mia were very lucky that Chet was the person to rediscover them.

After speaking to the organizers of the event, Ali gets approval to deliver a speech to the thousands in attendance along with the viewing audience of CNN and FOX News. The idea that mass numbers of people will hear and see her speak is daunting. Ali is full of resolve; her mission will be to focus on the real lives of Jilly and Mia. In her eyes and for the benefit of Chet, she will try to convey the real-life personalities of her sisters. Her goal becomes more than just having their names etched on a wall and forgotten.

On November 10th, the day before the ceremony, Cathy drives from her home in York, PA to take care of her father while Ali leaves for Washington. Cathy's husband, Carl, and their children will meet up with Ali and Chester's wife, Ann, and children at the Dupont Circle Hotel in the morning. The next morning at the hotel the absence of Chet, Chester, and Cathy are measurably noticeable. The attending family members have a strong will to carry out Chet's wishes. but can't help thinking about how the transplant operation will go. Chet's family is extremely torn between carrying out his wishes and being by his side during his operation.

Ali had no difficulty writing her speech, but was having a hard time coming to grips with how she would hold her composure as she spoke. Standing at a podium with generals and politicians while speaking to an audience of thousands doesn't seem to trouble Ali. But while only practicing her speech in front of a mirror, she begins to choke up just mentioning the three most important people in her life. The more she tries to rehearse, the more she is overcome with emotion. The only thing left for her to do was to pray to God for the strength so that she will be able to deliver a great speech.

While staring into the mirror, Ali begins to recall a happening in her past when she and Jilly were young girls. They were trying to hold their self-composure while reciting a passage together from The Book of Matthew. It was at their grandmother's funeral church mass in 1962. The church was packed with family and friends. Although the girls had practiced their lines over and over prior to the service, when it came to mentioning her grandmother by name Ali choked up and lost her composure. Jilly began to help her by explaining that she should mentally place her grandmother sitting in the front row, looking right in her eyes, and speak directly to her. Jilly's suggestion helped Ali to compose herself and finish her passage while visualizing her grandmother sitting in the front pew proudly smiling back at her.

On November 11th, an unmarked black shuttle bus is waiting outside the hotel which will transport Ali and Chet's family members to the Vietnam Women's Memorial at the National Mall in Washington, D.C. Everyone is aboard and has been waiting for ten minutes to leave when Ali asks the driver what's the hold up. The driver tells the group he is waiting for a the Metropolitan Police escort to arrive. A few minutes later the escort arrives, and they leave by way of Dupont Circle to New Hampshire Avenue then onto 23rd Street NW which takes them directly to the event in only ten minutes.

Pulling up to the Memorial with the Metro Police directing traffic, their shuttle bus is guided to an area marked off by police barricades. Once in the secured area, Ali looks out the bus window and notices CNN and Fox news satellite trucks with their roof top dishes pointed to the open skies. The bus stops to park, and the doors are opened when a National Parks person steps aboard and announces himself while asking all concerned to follow him. Everyone is guided to the front row which faces a stage and a podium with twelve empty chairs all lined up in a straight row.

Once they are seated, Ali feels a hand on her shoulder and hears a kind female voice ask her, "Are you Ali Parker?"

Ali turns her head and answers, "Yes, I am." The stranger introduces herself as Betty Santos and before she even tries to explain who she is, Ali says, "Oh, my God, I know who you are!" Ali reaches over to give Betty a hug and says, "Chet has told me so many good things about you. I feel as though you are part of my life!"

136

Betty replies, "I wish we were drawn together under more pleasant circumstances." Betty goes on to say, "I believe Mia and Jilly deserve to be honored here today, and I'm more than happy to be part of this." The National Parks person calls out Ali to take the center seat on the stage behind the podium. Ali asks Betty Santos to take her front row seat next to Chet's family members and introduces them to Betty. Ali, feeling a little more at ease, slowly walks toward the podium.

As Ali steps on to the stage, she notices the other seats beginning to fill in and within no more than a few more minutes, all participates are seated. Ali stares out into the audience, and she notices the contrast in attendees' attire ranging from businessmen, to military personnel, to emergency responders, as well as tattooed bikers. Looking through the prism of sunlight reflecting off the crowd, Ali begins to quiver as she realizes that people from all walks of life have come far and wide to honor her sisters. Ali glances over at Chet's family and notices Betty Santos giving her the thumbs up sign; Ali returns the gesture.

The PA system announces for everyone to stand for the presentation of the colors. From Ali's left side a small brigade of uniformed military members representing all the armed services, marching with their flags. Held in upright positions are The United States flag leading the way, POW/MIA, Marine Corps, Army, Navy, Air Force, and Coast Guard flags all proudly waving in the steady breeze. Once the honor guard are in place, The National Anthem is sung by The US Airforce Band. The combined music, lyrics, and rays of sun bouncing off the reflection pool of The National Mall causes many of the attendees to swallow hard and try hard to hold back their tears.

A call for a benediction by Colonel W.A. Turner is broadcast as all in attendance simultaneously lower their heads in prayer. The prayer is followed with a moment of silence for all those civilian volunteers who proudly gave their lives for their country. In the distance, half way between the Lincoln Memorial and the Vietnam Wall, is a lone standing bugler wearing a Navy full dress uniform playing the twenty-four notes of "Taps." There isn't a dry eye in sight as Ali tries to focus through her own tears on the face of an older white bearded man wearing a leather biker vest with numerous Vietnam Veteran patches. Ali then centers on the wrinkles of a biker veteran's face as the flow of tears run down his bearded cheeks, sending a message which takes her breathe away.

Ali Parker is introduced by a DOD Colonel, and she is requested to come to the podium, drawing the entire crowd to a deep silence. The few steps Ali had to take to reach the podium seemed like a hundred meters, leaving her feet to feel as though they were lined with lead. Ali finally takes the microphone and thanks the Women's Vietnam Veteran's Memorial for their efforts in honoring her sisters. Ali feels confident she has a well memorized speech, making her as ready as she will ever be. Ali's plan to openly share her sisters' lives with all attendees and television audience brings her a sense of relief as she realizes she will finally be relieving herself of a forty-year-old burden. Remembering Jilly's advice when speaking in public, Ali mentally places her sisters in the first row with Betty Santos between them. It is her intention to speak directly to Jilly and Mia hoping this will firmly hold her composure.

Meanwhile back in Kiawah Island, Chet and his son Chester are already prepped for surgery as they lie next to each other in the operating room at Roper Hospital. Chet tells Chester, "Remember your mother is here looking over us,"

Chester replies, "I already feel her presence, Dad." Silently to himself, Chet prays to God that nothing happens to his son and reaffirms his faith by accepting death for himself, but not his son. Dr. Graham has the anesthesiologist introduce sedation. As the father and son fall under the forces of anesthesia, Chet's daughter Cathy finds the softest available chair in the waiting room.

Standing tall while firmly holding onto her index cards, which contain her thoughts, Ali's beauty radiates out to the large crowd. Nothing can be heard except for the soft sound of the wind whirling around the Lincoln Memorial.

A loud and long-standing ovation is given by all attendees.

Ali begins her speech, "Thank you. Before I begin, I need to thank The Vietnam Women's Memorial, The Department of Defense, The Metropolitan Police, and all of you in attendance today for taking the time to remember two amazing young women.

Jill Landry and Mia Flynn were my sisters. Jill was my maternal sister and Mia, my informally adopted sister. It is very difficult for me to speak about my sisters and try to explain what their short-lived lives were like. They were part of my family, and we shared many of the same interests and principles. For me to convey their stories, I had to spiritually put on their shoes and walk in their footsteps.

I proudly stand here today watching the sun's reflection enhance the beautiful and captivating view of the Vietnam Women's Memorial sculpture behind us. The sculpture depicts a story of three nurses coming to aid a wounded soldier with nothing but sandbags for protection. Nowhere on the memorial will you find any names leaving us to make our own assumptions. Some of us have given those three young nurses the names of Faith, who is praying, Hope, who is looking toward heaven, and Charity, holding and protecting the soldier.

Just as those same three young women, my sisters had a calling and those calls were to be nurses. They kept their secret of volunteering for Vietnam from their own husbands. They were also trained and prepared to treat the most severe of injuries whether it be amputation, chemical burns, bullet, or shrapnel wounds. The need for them to serve their country was in great demand, and their potential to save many lives was lost forever.

Before it was even an idea to honor my sisters, Chet Ross, a Vietnam Veteran, also had a calling. His calling brought him back to a place he certainly wanted to forget, a place with terrible memories. Instead by returning, this calling lead him to find out answers which lead us to where we are today. Chet went to Vietnam as a stranger, but came home as a brother. He is now laying on a bed next to his son undergoing a liver transplant operation. Chet is fighting a tough fight against the effects of Agent Orange. I ask all of you to keep Chet Ross and his son Chester in your prayers. Chet is just like all the other Vietnam Veterans who asked for so little, but deserves so much more.

Jill and Mia were married a short time before arriving in Saigon. Jill's husband was George Wilkerson, and Mia's husband was John "Ricky" Ricciardi, both Air Force Veterans who also died in that senseless war. Both husband's names are etched on the great black granite wall behind us. They served together as bothers-in arms. They died together and now eternally sleep side-by-side in Arlington National Cemetery. We also have a solemn obligation to these two young men and the 58,218 other soldiers, sailors, and airmen who never had a chance to live the life most people take for granted.

My sisters were there when I needed them. They guided me so I wouldn't fall, gave me their shoulders to cry on, and laughter when I needed it. Most importantly Jilly and Mia are, and will always be, my best friends. Jill and Mia loved the Beatles and their music. Their favorite song was "In My Life." I quote from John Lennon's lyrics which sums up my sisters' lives:

"When I think, I know I'll never lose affection
For people and things that went before
I know I'll often stop and think about them
In my life, I love you more."

I often wondered as a young woman what it is about volunteering that makes it so rewarding. Jill and Mia volunteered for Vietnam service through the American Red Cross. I discovered that a volunteer doesn't volunteer because they hate what is in front of them. They volunteer because they love what they left behind. Volunteering allowed my sisters to abandon their lives for what they saw as a chance to be with their husbands. During the early years of the Vietnam War, there was a sense of patriotism. Women in the nursing profession were especially excited to go to war and use their skills.

The popular perception of women doing war work is that the men are in the danger zone, and the woman are safely behind them. That viewpoint has never been true and was certainly not true in Vietnam. My sisters were kidnapped in what was called a safe place, and we now know very well the enemy was everywhere. They were repeatedly beaten and tortured with no one to answer their screams for help.

Jilly and Mia were caged like animals and suspended over a muddy river where their captors would drop them to conceal their vulgar imprisonment. It took the forces of Mother Nature to sweep away and free my sisters from their captors and end their misery.

We all now look back upon the Vietnam War as something that happened a long time ago. But the truth is, long ago is never far away. For those of you who proudly served in the Vietnam War, being a veteran is a life sentence, and you live with it until the day you die. I thank you for answering the call of duty for an unappreciated war. Welcome Home!

My sisters died a horrible death witnessed by a young Vietnamese boy in 1968 who realized the importance of good versus evil. That boy's name is Ta Ning, and his tale was supported by finding my sisters dog tags and wedding band just before their captors abandoned them to drown in their cages. To all of us this should demonstrate the evils of war, forcing human beings to do unthinkable things against other human beings.

General Dwight Eisenhower once said there are two realities of War:

Try to forget them
but you never do.

My sisters died suddenly halfway around the world. I never got the chance to tell them that I loved them. Dying at a young age with most of their lives still ahead of them, Mia and Jill looked through a different prism in life than most of us are accustomed to. My family never received any statement or document showing the actual date of my sisters being killed. Unlike most who were killed in Vietnam, the surviving family members always know when their loved one was killed. My mom and dad died never knowing when tragedy struct their daughters.

Jilly and Mia were so alike in so many ways and enjoyed helping people whenever they had the chance. Being a nurse defines what my sisters were, and their devotion to the profession and each other was extraordinary.

An appropriate quote from Winston Churchill:

"It is war, viewed in its inherent quality, to establish on impregnable rocks, the right of the individual, and it is a war to establish and revive the stature of man. Perhaps it might seem a paradox that a war undertaken in the name of liberty and right should require, as a necessity of its process, the surrender for the time being of so many of the dearly valued liberties and rights"

As a great country, I hope we have learned from the mistakes of the Vietnam War and do not pass on these mistakes to future generations. Here are some words for thought, "We cannot control the wind, but we can control the sail."

To my sisters, I remember my first day without you both, and I've never been the same. You are still the angels of mercy in my eyes. When reflecting on the horrors of war, we rarely think of the toll it takes on the families back home. I ask you all to tell someone you love them today because tomorrow is not promised.

Behind every name on this wall is a hero who deserves to be remembered. There is always something to be thankful for. On behalf of my sisters, Jill Landry and Mia Flynn, thank you all for honoring them today, and God bless all the civilian volunteers who also gave their lives."

This was not an ordinary by the book speech, and the crowd warmly gives Ali a standing ovation as she walks off the stage toward Betty and Chet's family members. As the ceremony comes to the end, the entire family is thanked by dignitaries along their walk back to the black bus. Ali asks Betty if she would like to ride with her on the bus back to The Dupont Hotel, and Betty accepts the invitation. With the help of The Metro Police, they all board the bus while keeping the news media at bay. All this commotion and fuss reassured Ali that Jilly and Mia are now known heroes who will not easily be forgotten, and that's all that matters.

On the ride back to The Dupont Hotel, Ali thanks Betty for being such a vital part in getting her sisters' story told. Ali asks Betty, "There is one thing in my mind that is bothering me, and just maybe you can help?"

Betty replies, "And what is that?

Ali asks, "Only one white gold wedding band was found which belonged to Jilly. Would you happen to know where Mia's yellow gold wedding band is?" Just as Betty is ready to speak, the bus comes to a halt, and the bus driver announces their arrival at The Dupont. Once inside the hotel lobby, Ali says her goodbyes to the family and motions Betty to take a seat on the nearest couch. At first Betty seems taken back by Ali's questioning about the where-abouts of Mia's ring, but she begins to realize it may have an important meaning to her.

Betty assumes that Ali is aware of the small part she played in her sister's disappearance. She explains that her conversation that she had with Mia and Jilly was only over a span of maybe an hour. As Betty is speaking she realizes why Ali thinks she may know something important about the missing ring. Betty tries to cover her mouth, but still spits out the words, "Oh my, I was the last person to see or speak to Mia and Jilly!" Lost for words, Betty can only say that she was devastated when she discovered that the girls did not return that dreadful night. Betty reaches into her handbag for a tissue, wipes her tears and says, "I wish I had an answer for you about the ring, but I unfortunately don't."

Ali answers, "I didn't think so. After what my sisters went through, that ring could be anywhere". Betty and Ali stand up, give each other a hug, and agreed to keep in touch. As they start to walk away from each other, Betty says, "I see so much of Jilly in your eyes."

Ali utters, "My mom always told me that too."

Ali rushes to her room so she can call Cathy and check in on Chet and Chester. Cathy picks up on the first ring and advises Ali that all went well in the operation room, and her father and brother are now in the recovery room. Cathy tells Ali that Dr. Graham and Dr. Carter seems to feel that they removed all the mass and replaced it with enough tissue so that Chet will make a full recovery. Dr. Carter also said that the danger period is not totally over, but he is hopeful that Chet's body will not reject the transplant. Ali is delighted to hear the news and decides to immediately get ready to drive back to Kiawah Island. It was Cathy's plan to sit and wait in the recovery room until her father and brother woke up from the anesthesia. Ali is aware that Kiawah Island is about a nine-hour drive and tells Cathy she will be leaving as soon as she checks out of the hotel. Before they hang up, Cathy expresses how great Ali's speech was and that Fox News had a lot of nice things to say about the event. Ali expresses to Cathy that she wished she had asked her to record the event when Cathy replies, "All done. My father would have killed me if I didn't record it."

Ali replies, "Oh, thank God!"

Ali senses a weird feeling and plans on driving straight through the night so she can get to Chet as soon as she can. Crazy thoughts keep running around in Ali's mind. The drive feels like she is travelling at slow speed although she is cruising well over seventy-five miles per hour. Hardly ever leaving the left lane, Ali passes all types of vehicles while hoping not to be stopped for speeding. Only a one planned pit stop for a quick check in call to Cathy, fuel, and a slice of pizza at a rest area in North Carolina separate her from getting to Chet.

At about 10:00 pm, Ali pulls into the driveway of Roper Hospital and senses her feelings of guilt for leaving Chet fade. Still in the back of her mind, she feels that being at his side would have been the proper thing to do. But doing what she did for her sisters meant more to her, while also making Chet happy. Entering through the main front entrance, Ali quickly notices Cathy sitting on a chair facing a giant fish tank. The only sound that could be heard was an occasional hospital page and the sound of bubbles churning to the surface of the fish tank. Cathy lifts her head, allowing Ali to see her happy tears, and tells her that her father and brother are fine and sleeping. Ali drops to her knees and rests her head in Cathy's lap. While petting Ali's head, Cathy tells her that just thirty minutes ago, Chet opened his eyes and smiled at her. The nurse then came into the room and gave him a sedative to assure he went back to asleep. Cathy explained that she then bundled him up with blankets, stared dreamily into her eyes, and shortly fell back to sleep.

Cathy mentions to Ali that she thought she heard Chet talking to himself or on the phone just before the doctors prepped him for surgery. It appeared to Cathy that he was having a conversation with someone, but Cathy then thought he might have been praying, so she didn't want to disturb him. When the talking seemed to stop, she went to check on him, but the medication had already taken effect, and he was sound asleep. Cathy asks Ali, "Was he talking to you on the phone?"

Ali said, "No, Cathy, it wasn't me."

Ali wandered her way up to the third-floor and room number 311 and caught her first glimpse of Chet sleeping. She walked over and stood behind his wheeled service cart as though she wanted him to see her first after awakening. Gradually Ali circles Chet and slowly slides her chair closer so she can hold his hand. When she finally touches his hand, she feels that it is cool to her touch. Spreading his hand open thinking it will warm it, Ali notices the dog tags and wedding band clutched in his right hand. Sticking halfway open is a draw which catches her eye. She fully opens the draw and sees a photo of Chet's pennant blue 1954 Corvette convertible, an old 1940's Esterbrook fountain pen, and a picture of her and Chet taken at the Riptide restaurant. Ali takes the items in her hands, tells him that she loves him and always will, and kisses his forehead.

When she holds up the dog tags, Ali notices something strange. She now sees two wedding bands linked together within the same chain and an old American Red Cross pin tangled in the chain. The missing yellow gold wedding band with the inscription "Love always, Ricky" is suddenly in the palm of her hand! For a moment, Ali questions herself thinking she might be hallucinating. Tears begin to run down her face, but Ali desperately tries to wipe them dry to get a better look at the yellow gold ring. She knows damn well the ring has been missing and is absolutely astonished by its sudden appearance. Ali holds up the ring to the light so she can get a better view to read the inscription. Ali reads and hears the words spoken as though it was Ricky himself, "Love always, Ricky." Until now Ali always looked at the world in a realistic manner. Suddenly she believes there just might be unexplainable forces at work. How did the second wedding band get here? Recalling Chet's daydream of having a conversation with Jilly and Mia is now believed by Ali as something that must have taken place. Perhaps Cathy did hear Chet having a conversation with someone in his hospital room. Did Ali's sisters pay a visit to Chet while he was waiting for surgery to let him know that they are now in a good place? Was it Mia and Jilly who left the ring? Now there are more unanswered questions in Ali's mind that need to be answered.

A nurse enters the room to check on Chet and asks Ali if there is anything she could do. The nurse tells her that there are sofas in the third-floor visitor's room that will make it much more pleasant to sleep. Ali replies, "No, thank you." She makes herself as comfortable as possible by placing an extra pillow in front of her and leans her head and shoulders at the foot of Chet's bed. She is exhausted. It has been a very long day.

Chapter 12

2006 Las Vegas, NV

The sunlight is beginning to creep between the open crack of the hotel curtains, and a strong ray of warm light is now shinning on her slightly wrinkled face. It only was just a few hours ago that she fell asleep after another long night of singing old songs she no longer enjoyed singing. She still sells out each performance wherever she goes, and the crowds scream and chant for more. Hidden behind all the fame and fortune is a lonely woman who now yearns for what she pushed aside in her early life a long time ago. It didn't take long for her career to skyrocket to the top, sharing her stunning voice with her fans worldwide. At her home in California, she has recently packed away many boxes of awards ranging from Grammy, Golden Globe, Tony, and Country Music Awards. Last year she was even voted into The Rock and Roll Hall of Fame and starred on Broadway in the 1980's. Her forty years on stage was shared with some of the best singer and song writers in the business, including Jackson Browne, Neil Young, James Taylor, and The Eagles.

Her performing years are now officially over, and last night's show was her last due to health conditions she no longer can control. She has been told by her doctors that under the best of conditions she has two years before her progressive movement disorder will worsen to the point of strangling her normal brain functions. The "P" word, Parkinson's, now stands between her and her unfortunate imminent future. She is now forced to find the strength and drive to get her life together and make the best of what little time she has left.

Her tired worn-out body finally finds the strength to get out of bed as she wraps herself in a plush terry-cloth hotel robe with an embroidered coat of arms of The Bellagio Hotel and Casino on the left breast pocket. She grabs the TV remote and walks toward the panoramic window of her presidential suite. She then proceeds to open the curtains very slowly so her eyes can adjust to the warm, vivid light. Once the curtains are fully opened, she has the most spectacular view of the city of Las Vegas, and the hustle and bustle in the streets below living up to its slogan "The city that never sleeps."

Her eyes begin to scan the vast landscape and hotel surroundings as she looks over the famous Las Vegas Strip with a full lake view acting as though it was a buffer to separate her from her past. In the far distance, she can see planes approaching the airport and envisions how it was many years ago when she began her career in the late 1960's. Her eyes begin to retract and suddenly stop to focus on the Bellagio's huge one hundred and fifty-foot-high marquee which still reads "Final Show: Sharon Onstadt Farewell Tour." Sharon takes a few steps back, firmly presses the power button on the TV remote, and scans a few channels looking for the news of the day, stopping when she reaches CNN.

Sharon raises the volume and decides to listen while she showers, leaving the bathroom door wide open. The unique bathroom has been constructed from special imported Italian marble on the floor and walls reflecting a white base with streaks of purple, blue and black veins. As Sharon gradually turns on the shower and waits for the right lukewarm temperature, she hears a special report from The Vietnam Women's Memorial in Washington, D.C. She overhears something about two MIA Red Cross nurses who are, after forty years, finally being honored. Not yet wet, Sharon decides to step out of the shower and again wrap herself in her robe as she walks closer to the TV in the living room. The CNN field reporter mentions that a sister of the two MIA nurses named Ali Parker will be the guest speaker. At the bottom of the TV screen, Sharon reads the news banner and catches the names of Mia Flynn and Jill Landry flashing before her eyes.

Sharon always wondered if Mia and Jilly ever took her advice to stop down playing the dangers of war. She had an odd feeling back in 1968 when the three of them said their final goodbyes at Clark Airforce Base. Something very bizarre made Sharon believe that Mia and Jilly wouldn't follow her suggestion to call their husbands. It was Sharon's belief that speaking to their husbands would have persuaded them from going and return home. The fact that they never did call their husbands is confirmed when Sharon hears Ali mention it in her speech along with the terrifying news that they, along with their husbands, were among the casualties of the Vietnam war.

Sharon's body begins to tremble and tears start to flow down her cheeks as she recalls how lucky in a way Mia and Jilly were married to the loves of their lives and so much in love. In her own past, Sharon gave up marrying at a young age and starting a family for an entertainment career. She realizes that not having any family at this stage in her life was a big mistake that she now must live with. Those boxes of awards don't mean anything to her now, and she would gratefully trade them in for a family she could call her own.

In 1977 when she was ready to settle down, the love of her life, Jimmy Baxter, was already happily married with two children. That immense disappointment in her life kept her void of the need to find another deep love which she now sincerely regrets. Her past love life was filled with dating and in a few instances engagements to some famous men who never came close to her Jimmy. Through it all, the former "American Red Cross Donut Dolly" Sharon Onstadt did fulfill her lifelong dream to become one of the world's best-selling recording artists of all time.

Feeling a huge void in her life, Sharon decides it is important for her to give back in some way. She realizes that her time as a Donut Dolly meant a great deal to her and was an integral part of her becoming a well renown entertainer. Giving back is a way for her to fill her void. In doing so she hopes that she can also be remembered as a philanthropist and not only an entertainer.

Chapter 13

2006 Kiawah, SC

Thunder sends its vibrating sounds rattling the walls and building as the hospital lights briefly flicker. Heavy rain begins to fall sideways by a robust wind slamming against the hospital room windows. The loud noises don't seem to bother her because she is in a deep sleep.

Doctor Carter walks into Chet's hospital room and notices Ali soundly asleep at the foot of the bed. Doctor Carter gently wakes Ali up by tapping on her shoulder. Ali is startled and for a moment doesn't know where she is. At first she focuses on checking her surroundings as she catches a glance of Chet who is still asleep. Her neck is stiff, and her back is aching as she tries to straighten up and loosen her rigid muscles. Finally, Ali remembers being totally exhausted the night before and falling asleep at the foot of the bed. Doctor Carter says, "Good morning, Ali."

Doctor Carter wakes up Chet while checking his vital signs at each of the connected monitors and adjusts the intravenous flow of liquid. Chet's eyes are now open as he cracks a smile, and Ali walks to the head of the bed and gives him a kiss on his forehead. Ali says, "Good morning, how are you feeling?"

In a gravel tone voice, Chet replies, "Okay, but I'm very thirsty." Ali looks toward Doctor Carter for approval, and he nods his head yes. Chet is then propped up, and Ali pours a glass of water from a nearby pitcher. Doctor Carter continues to check Chet's medical charts for anything out of the ordinary while Ali and Chet patiently wait for the doctor's comments.

Doctor Carter tells Chet that everything looks good right now, and it seems that Chet's body is accepting the new liver tissue. Chet asks, "How long do I have to be here?"

Doctor Carter replies, "About a week or so." The good news revitalizes Chet and Ali's spirts as their facial expressions display two big smiles. Chet asks, "Doctor, how is my son Chester doing?" The doctor explains that he is doing excellent, and his body is already showing signs of healing.

"Since Chester doesn't have any transplanted tissue, there is no chance of rejection, and he should be released a few days before you. I have already made arrangements to have Chester moved into this room so you both can at least be together."

Ali answers. "That's great news, Doctor Carter. Thank you so much."

Doctor Carter says, "I have another patient who needs my attention. I'll drop by tomorrow and if the nursing staff needs me, they know how to find me." The doctor turns and leaves the room waving his hand goodbye.

At last they are alone when Ali tells Chet that she missed him while she was in Washington and was very worried about the outcome of the operation. Ali admits that during her stay in Washington, she couldn't help but constantly think about Chet and Chester. Hearing Doctor Carter's words of recovery make her extremely happy that all the bad is mostly in the past now. Chet tells her that he is so proud of her for delivering the speech, and he can't wait to watch it when he gets home on his VCR. Even though Chet hasn't viewed the speech, he tries to explain that when reading it before his surgery it gave him goose bumps. Everything Chet would have said in his own words was clearly covered in Ali's speech, and he could not have done a better job than her. Chet says, "Being a sister of Jilly and Mia helped carry your speech with much more weight than I could have ever delivered."

Ali remarks, "Thank you, Chet, now I can't wait to see how I look on TV," and Chet responds, "Very beautiful, I'm sure."

Ali now considers it a good time to bring up the reappearance of the missing wedding band. She says, "Chet, I noticed in the draw next to you the dog tags with two wedding bands chained together and an American Red Cross Pin. It looks like it's Mia's missing ring?" Chet asks Ali to go in the drawer and give him the dog tags and wedding bands. Ali places everything into the palm of Chet's hand as he closely examines what Ali has told him. Chet pulls out and holds up the yellow gold band and reads the inscription out loud, "Love Always, Ricky." Silently Chet pauses as though in deep thought while Ali waits for a reply.

Chet to conclude says, "It must have been Ta, who else could have done this? That son of a gun somehow did find it. It's all too much for me to comprehend."

Ali asks, "Is Ta here in Kiawah?" Chet explains that just prior to his being prepped for surgery, he received a call from Ta. Ali replies, "That must have been who you were talking to when Cathy heard voices from your room. She thought it might have been you praying so she didn't disturb you." Chet mentions that Ta was recently in Atlanta on his way to Montana. Ali says, "What's in Montana?"

Chet says, "I don't know. We had to quickly end our phone call after I told him I was on my way to the operating room, but he did mention that he had some good news for me." Ali is now feeling a little better about the missing ring and begins to tell Chet she thought it might have reappeared by a spiritual force. Chet agrees with Ali and tells her under the circumstances he would have thought the same thing, but he still feels that some kind of special forces have lead him to meet her and the place where Mia and Jilly died.

A nurse suddenly walks into the room pushing a small wheeled cart with a liquid breakfast for Chet who makes a squeamish face when he takes a sniff. Ali tells Chet that she must freshen up and get something to eat herself when the nurse recommends the cafeteria downstairs on the ground floor. Ali gives Chet another kiss on his forehead and laughingly says, "Enjoy your breakfast. I'll see you in a little bit."

About an hour later, Ali returns to the room and notices a slender Asian man talking to Chet. In the corner of his eye, Chet notices Ali in the doorway and announces, "Ta, I want you to meet Ali. Ali, this is Ta."

Still surprised that Ta is in Kiawah, she says, "It's an honor to meet you; I've heard so many good things about you, and I would like to thank you for what you have done for my sisters." Being the humble person he is, Ta replies, "You are welcome, and I have to say that your speech was excellent. I watched it live on CNN while at the San Francisco Airport, and I can tell you it caught the attention of many traveling passengers."

Ta apologizes for shocking Ali and Chet by placing the missing ring in the drawer last night without any note. Ta explains that about 8 pm last night he came into the hospital room while Chet was sleeping. He sat in a chair and prayed awhile for Chet's recovery. While Ta was praying, he observed the drawer next to the bed was slightly open when he noticed the dog tags and white gold wedding band chained together. The night nurse rushed into the room asked him his name, which she checked on a list and told him he wasn't an authorized family member. Ta was then told by the night nurse to leave, so he did and figured he would be back in the morning.

Chet says to Ta, "Please tell us how you found the missing ring and the American Red Cross pin?" Ta begins by telling Ali and Chet that after his phone conversation with Chet concerning a dream about Mia and Jilly riding in Chet's car. Something hit me when Chet said, "Mia told me she swallowed her ring before the Viet Cong had a chance to take it away. That was when I knew it had to be in or around the hut where the girls were kept prisoners."

Ali asks, "What made you think that?"

And Ta replies, "If it was swallowed by Mia, then it had to be passed by Mia." Ta gives a horrendous description of sanitary conditions while the girls were prisoners. All waste was dumped in deep holes which the girls themselves were forced to dig. Ta explains that some of the holes were three or four feet deep, and he knew some sort of metal detection would be needed.

A few days later after the conversation with Chet and his dream, Ta recruited five other surviving orphans of the war and asked them to join his team in finding the missing ring. Ta was able to obtain a state of the art metal detector which had the ability to find small metal objects as far down as four feet in the ground. Ta realized that area to be searched was going to be large; he needed a detailed plan before proceeding. Prior to starting the search, Ta and his team visited the site and staked out ground markings with yellow caution tape using the closest layout of the land that Ta still had fixed in his memory. Many of the old structures were washed away during Typhoon Cobra which made the search much more problematic. It was very difficult to get a good idea of exactly where each hut was since forty years of time had passed. Between Ta and the others combined, their thorough memories of the village were fortunately still fresh in their minds just as though it might have been yesterday.

Even with the metal detector, locating the wedding band didn't come easy for the team of searchers. While digging they found hundreds of metal objects within a close vicinity and practically had to dig up the entire site. Ta and his team used sifters to go through each shovel full of earth and run it by the metal detector. Some of the more popular items that were found during the search were unused bullets, empty cartridges, empty k-ration cans, and grenade pins.

Ta describes that many hot and humid days of hard labor passed by without finding anything pertinent. Ta declares, "We all realized that the ring was a very important missing piece to a puzzle."

On the tenth day just when the team seemed discouraged, we found the American Red Cross pin which gave us the feeling that we were very close. It made our work effort more intense as though a force from beyond allowed us to find that pin. Ta says, "Who else could the pin belong to? It had to belong to one of the girls." Another two days went by before we heard a solid loud beep on the metal detector and as we sifted through the muck, a shining gold ring suddenly appeared. We rinsed it off with clean water which made the inscription clearly visible, and I then read it to the team, "Love always, Ricky." Reading those three words out loud to the team made them feel accomplished. Chet being very quiet, Ali says, "On behalf of Jilly and Mia, thank you and your team for giving me some sort of closure. I don't know how to repay you."

Ta utters the words, "Witnessing the happy expressions on both your faces is more than enough payment."

Being a good listener, Chet says, "What brings you to the United States, and how does Montana fit into all this?" Ta enlightens Chet and Ali of his new job with The National Alliance of Families (NAF) based in Billings, Montana. While Ta and his team were digging at the old marina, the word got out that they were trying to locate belongings of two missing American Red Cross nurses who disappeared during the war. Ta was contacted by the (NAF) who wanted to know if he was interested working with the NAF in finding missing-in-action personnel in Vietnam and neighboring countries. Ta details that NAF was founded in 1990 which had its original roots with The National League of Families of American Prisoners and Missing who first established the now famous black and white POW/MIA flag which flies under the United States flag. Ta proudly says, "I convinced them before I accepted the position to include all American civilians who went missing in the Vietnam War, and they agreed by allowing me to oversee all digging sites."

Ta continues saying, "Now I hope that explains what brought me to the US, and it just so happened that when I saw Ali giving her speech on TV and hearing my name mentioned, I decided to call Chet. It was my original plan to fly out to Billings and on the return, stop and see you. But after that quick call to Chet made me change my itinerary to fly to Charleston to be here when you came out of recovery."

Chet replies, "How long can you stay here in Kiawah? I have a big empty house, and you are more than welcome."

Explaining his tight schedule, Ta must be in Billings for a dinner meeting that night, and he already has his first official assignment to commence next week in Vietnam. He seems very anxious and explains that he needs a few days before beginning to assemble a team and lay out his new plans. Ta mentions that he is all packed and ready for his flight to Billings, and a prearranged taxi will be showing up in fifteen minutes outside the hospital to take him to the Charleston airport. Chet asks Ta for a favor, to make a quick stop and introduce himself to his son Chester on the second floor who would be very happy to meet him. Ali jumps in and says, "I'll show you to his room and introduce you. Chester will love it."

Ta promises to keep in touch and offers Chet and Ali to come visit him since he will be looking for good volunteers to help those families who are still waiting for their loved ones to return home. Ali says, "We just might take you up on your offer." Chet extends his right hand, and Ta gives him his as they shank hands while Ta remarks, "Till we meet again, my friend."

Ali speaks up saying, "Follow me, Ta, let's go meet Chester."

A week later, Chet's son Chester has already been released, and Chet is once again alone in his hospital room. Ali just arrived in Chet's room carrying an empty box and has a funny look on her face. Chet asks, "You seem to be in a really happy mood, just as though you swallowed a canary." Ali is about to comment, but is interrupted when Doctor Carter drops by to advise Chet that he will be released in the morning. The news brings a tremendous amount of joy to Chet who has just about reached his limits as a patient. The freedom and the thought of finally being in his own home and sleeping in his own bed sparks a rejuvenation of his desire to never again take for granted those little things in life.

Doctor Carter gives Ali a few prescriptions that need to be filled as soon as possible and a list of certain foods Chet should not eat. The doctor advises

Chet that he has an appointment next Thursday at his office for a follow up visit and to take it easy when he gets home. Ali says, "Doctor Carter, please put me in charge, and I'll make sure he follows your orders."

The doctor replies, "Ali, you are now in charge."

Once at home, it doesn't take Chet long to get reacquainted with his familiar surroundings as he is finally able to slowly walk to his deck to absorb the beautiful ocean views. Ali and Chet now find the time to watch the recorded speech given by Ali at the Vietnam Women's Memorial in Washington and are both joyous by the reported news coverage of the event. Ali says, "I don't know what gave me the strength to deliver those words to that enormous audience in attendance and watching on TV."

Chet responds with teary eyes, "I know where your courage came from; it came from the two most important people in your life that gave you the needed willpower."

Chet is reacquainted with one of his favorite pastimes, sitting in his preferred deck chair watching the clouds and seagulls flying by. While sitting on his deck, Chet now has the chance to add some color to his pale complexion. At first Ali is always by his side making sure he doesn't fall and as each day passes, Chet's ability extends further and further. By the second week at home, Chet can manage short early morning strolls with Ali on the beach while they feed the seagulls and sand pipers.

Six weeks has passed since Chet has been home and by now he is ninety-nine percent back into feeling his old self. Ali has been doing the food shopping and on this morning, she left at 10 am, and it's been over four hours since she left. The local grocery store is only a ten minute drive from the house, and Chet is beginning to worry. He doesn't want to be embarrassed to call her and find out her being late was something she told him, and he didn't pay addition to what she said. Another half an hour passes, and Chet finally decides to call Ali who doesn't answer as he reluctantly leaves a message to call him back.

At last Chet hears the front door open while he is still resting in bed followed by the usual sounds of slamming of cabinet doors and the refrigerator opening and closing. Ali continues to put away the groceries. Chet unexpectedly hears a strange unfamiliar thumping sound that excites his curiosity. However, Chet brushes away the strange sound and for the moment is more inquisitive to know what took Ali so long to return home from the local grocery store. The sounds of shuffled groceries begin to diminish except for the thumping sound. Chet is anxious to know what took Ali so long at the grocery store and why she didn't return his call.

Chet finally hears Ali climbing the stairs and as she reaches the second-floor, Chet hears her say in a whispering voice, "Come on, come on, boy!" The master bedroom door swiftly opens when Chet catches the view of Ali holding in her arms a puppy chocolate lab. Ali kiddingly says, "Look what I found on the beach, and his name is Buck!"

Chapter 14

2006 Kiawah Island, SC

Life often surprises us when evil forces overshadow the good. The darkness of evil is never in permanent control and over time, it will slowly be eliminated by the good.

Six months after Mia and Jilly were honored by The Women's Vietnam Memorial, Ali was contacted by the Cities of Quincy, IL and Peshtigo, WI whose mayors wanted to posthumously honor their hometown heroines. Once the arrangements were made, Ali and Chet flew to St. Louis, MO and attended two separate ceremonies one day apart. Mia was honored with a park in the City of Quincy named "Mia Flynn Park." Jilly was honored by the City of Peshtigo by having the street she grew up on "Eagle Street" officially changed to "Jill Landry Boulevard."

The next two years rolled by quickly as Chet, Ali, and their new addition, Buck, continued to live their lives to the fullest. Customary strolls along the beach are still a favorite pastime of Ali and Chet. But times have again changed. Instead of feeding the seagulls and sandpipers, they are watching Buck bark and chase birds. Ali now prefers tossing a stick out over the water and watching

Buck swim and swiftly retrieve it. Buck never shows any sign of exhaustion and keeps on barking for more of Ali's tosses. Life is good for the couple as they strive to fully enjoy the important little things life has to offer.

Ta and Chet make it a point to call each other at least twice a year during the Tet (January) and Thanksgiving holidays. Both men enjoy bringing one another up to date in each of their own lives. Ta is doing well with The National Alliance of Families, and he usually tries to make the trip to the United States every year. So far Ta and his team have found the remains of two missing people who served in the Vietnam War as civilians. The first to be found was Brad Perot of Tampa, FL who was a missionary volunteer. Ta's recent second recovery was Janet Grossman of Stratford, CT who was a field contract worker employed by her hometown-based Sikorsky Helicopter Company. Janet's vanishing was frightfully like Mia and Jilly's disappearance since it took place in Saigon around the same time. Just like Mia and Jilly, Janet Grossman was last seen walking into a bar on Tu Do Street in Old Saigon. Janet was innocently trying to celebrate her twenty-first birthday. Ta now firmly believes that the similarities between the three girls gone missing is no coincidence.

Ali has taken an early retirement from Carver Yachts after turning down a newly created position to manage their east coast sales operation. Though the job would have only covered the Boston to Washington, D.C. area, she realized that traveling away from Kiawah, even for a few days a week, was still too much for her and Chet to accept. Chet and Ali strategically planned to travel overseas at least for a few months a year and working would have been a big obstacle to those plans. Chet needed Ali to be fully retired to accomplish their travel and retirement plans. Packing her personal effects in Peshtigo and moving to Kiawah wasn't as easy as Ali thought. Saying her final goodbyes to her friends and co-workers was much tougher than she expected. After all the years of living in Peshtigo, Ali never gave up hope that one day there would be a knock on her door and when she answered, her sisters would be there. Ali finds it very difficult saying goodbye to the same people that helped her the most during her family tragedy. Facing her friends and knowing that it would probably be the last time they will see each other again was not easy to do.

Ali decided early in her adult life to stay in the town that was more than just a homebased memory, it also was a foundation rooted in her life. Ali fondly remembers the times when her parents would take her and Jilly ice skating on the nearby lake after church on Sundays. On the way home from the lake, her father

Dave would ask his daughters, "Does anyone feel like having pancakes?" which always received a fast response from Ali and Jilly, "Yes, Daddy, we do!" Dave would then steer the family car towards the International House of Pancakes knowing that they must return home before the Green Bay Packers game came on TV.

Chet also travelled to Peshtigo with Ali and tried to give her the added support she needed while she packed up her life into boxes. Chet placed himself in Ali's shoes on a few occasions and knew this would not a be an easy task to just pick up and leave. Chet knew this was the first time in her life that she officially left the city that shielded her from her family tragedy and her parents passing away. Before leaving Ali made a list of the people who really meant something special to her, and she made it a point that no one on that list was missed in receiving her personal goodbyes. It took three long and difficult days for Ali to track down each of her special friends and by the time she was finished, Ali was emotionally drained.

On an overcast Kiawah morning, thunderstorms were expected to arrive by noon when Chet and Ali notice black and blue skies rapidly approaching ahead of schedule. They decide not to take their usual morning stroll in fear of lightning which is flaring up in the not too far distance. Instead Chet and Ali decide on making their next vacation plans. Ali would love to travel this year to Hawaii. Chet agrees he would too, but also likes Australia as a possibility. Ali has already sent away for a Hawaiian tour booklet from Perillo Tours and hands it to Chet for his opinion. Chet is not sure if a tour is the way to go and suggests maybe a direct booking on their own would best suit their needs. Ali reminds Chet that neither of them have ever been to Hawaii or know anyone who has, so picking and planning a trip would be taking a chance. Chet says, "I'm sure there isn't a bad place in Hawaii to stay, so what's all the worry about?"

Ali replies, "But a tour will guarantee us we will not miss any important points of interest in wherever we stay."

Just as Chet is about to answer Ali, his cell phone rings, and he notices Ta's name in the caller ID, and the call is coming from Vietnam. Chet answers the call by saying, "Hello, my friend! What makes you call in the month of April?"

Ta answers, "I thought you may still be interested to know something. Do you and Ali still want to visit Vietnam because I just received some important information concerning a missing nineteen-year-old woman who went missing a week after Jilly and Mia." Chet tells Ta that he will put his phone on speaker so Ali can listen in and to repeat what he just said.

Ta is upset as he closely describes his new case file that was just handed to him involving a young journalist who went missing on July 5, 1968. The women's name is Dorothy Chase who worked for two years at United Press International as a news correspondent covering the war. Her hometown was Flagstaff, AZ, and she was also last seen in the downtown area of Old Saigon the night of July 5th. For the last twenty-five years, Dorothy's brother has been trying to find out what happened to his sister on that frightful night. The similarities of Dorothy's case file are again too close for Ta to accept as just a coincidence. Chet, feeling shocked himself when hearing the case resemblances, asks Ta, "How come the police at the time didn't pick up on this?"

Ta replies, "A corrupt police detective named Chi was paid off to keep the disappearances silent, and I have more information that will turn your stomach sick."

Ta goes on further to describe the unscrupulous characters involved in a secret cover-up of kidnapping and human trafficking. It all begins with a bartender named Bao Hue who worked at a placed called the Blue Oyster Bar during 1968. Ta mentions that he remembers the bar as a young teenager being a seedy place to never go into. Most of the bars on Tu Do Street also fit the same description. Ta informs Chet and Ali that recently, on his own merit, Bao walked into police headquarters to confess his taking part in a horrible conspiracy. After over forty years of living with the guilt, he finally came to realize that the seriousness of the crimes is now too much for him to bear. Bao has given the police some very stunning information about what was going on at the suspicious Blue Oyster Bar. Bao, who was at the time a young man, saw many Caucasian women who individually or in pairs visited the bar and were drugged by a sleazy guy called Lanh Phu who is now in his seventies. Chet says, "Did you say pairs?"

Ta replies, "Yes, in pairs! And I also firmly believe my new case of Dorothy Chase, as well as those of Janet Grossman, Mia Flynn, and Jilly Landry, were commandeered by the same group of people." Ali is shocked and finds it difficult to speak and can only whisper, "Oh, my God!"

Continuing the conversation, Ta explains that Bao admits that he also was paid by Lanh to look the other way whenever a powdery substance was added to women's drinks. When confessing Bao made it clear to the police that if he didn't go along with the scheme, he would have been killed. Ta says, "Are you ready for this? Bao is willing to testify against Lanh in court."

Ali asks, "Ta, how did you find out all this?"

Ta answers, "One of my part time volunteers who helped me locate the missing wedding band is a decorated police office in Ho Chi Minh City, and he quietly gave me a copy of the files. That's not all, The National Alliance of Families has recently received a $500,000 special donation from an individual named Sharon Onstadt. Her donation directive is to use the funds for finding missing volunteers during the Vietnam War. By the way, her donation was in memory of Mia Flynn and Jill Landry! Do you guys know who Sharon Onstadt is?"

Chet and Ali reply, "Yes, she is a famous singer songwriter who recorded award winning albums especially during the 1970's and 80's. But we have no idea of her connection or why she would make such a large donation."

Ta responds, "Ali, I think it's a remarkable connection to you and not just a fluke. Somehow your speech in Washington opened a special door in the past that needed to be closed and in my mind, Mia and Jilly's paths somehow crossed with Sharon Onstadt."

Chet asks Ta, "Is it time for us to come to Vietnam?"

Ali jumps in and says, "Ta, is your offer still open for us to come?"

Ta replies, "Yes, it is! The sooner you get here the better and by the way, I have been told that the sleazy guy named Lanh is still alive and in police custody."

Ta declares some more good news by saying, "I have also been told by officials that there is no statute of limitations under international law for genocide, crimes against humanity, and war crimes. The police will hand this case over to the Republic for handling."

Chet wants Ta to know that they were just planning a vacation to Hawaii, and his call was perfectly timed. Ali explains that they must make arrangements with Chet's daughter Cathy to take in Buck while they are away. Chet mentions that they have some other little things to clear up first before leaving and finishes by saying, "After all these years, this guy Linh somehow managed to live a full life as a free man, but now must pay the price."

Ali's final remark to Ta is, "I need to look Lanh straight into his eyes and tell him that all those women he robbed from their families are now reaching out from their graves to make sure he rots in hell."

Ta graciously responds, "Ali, I think we can arrange that."

The end……

References

"In My Life" Lyrics by John Lennon / Paul McCartney
"No More Vietnams" by Richard Nixon